Christ and Power

Martin Hengel

CHRIST and POWER

translated by Everett R. Kalin

FORTRESS PRESS   Philadelphia

This book is a translation of *Christus und die Macht. Die Macht Christi und die Ohnmacht der Christen. Zur Problematik einer "Politischen Theologie" in der Geschichte der Kirche,* copyright © 1974 by Calwer Verlag Stuttgart in Germany.

Biblical quotations from the Revised Standard Version of the Bible, copyrighted 1946, 1952, © 1971, 1973 by the Division of Christian Education of the National Council of the Churches of Christ in the U.S.A., are used by permission.

Library of Congress Catalog Card Number 76–62608
ISBN 0–8006–1256–6

6179J76   Printed in U.S.A.   1–1256

Contents

Preface   vii

Introduction: The Problem of Christ and Power   1

1. Concerning the History-of-Religions Problem of Power   5

2. Concerning Political Religion in Antiquity   7

3. Theocracy and Ancient Judaism   11

4. Jesus of Nazareth and the Powers of His Time   15

5. Power and Powerlessness in the Early Church   23

6. The Power of the State and the Authority
of the Community   33

7. Toward the Establishment of the Imperial Church   51

8. The Two Kingdoms or the Reign of Christ   69

Summary   81

Preface

This brief study served as the basis for a lecture I gave at a meeting of the *Paulusgesellschaft* in Bad Godesberg in 1972. It has been reworked and extensively enlarged. I have avoided extensive footnoting, other than to give the sources of all quotations. Foreign language quotations and concepts have been translated wherever possible. I ask the indulgence of the specialists for forsaking in this study the narrow confines of my discipline, which is the New Testament and its Jewish and Hellenistic-Roman environment, and for pushing forward into other fields—much disputed ones at that. An ever-increasing specialization exists in theology as in other fields. Thus one should endeavor to produce not only narrow technical studies but also comprehensive overviews, especially when it is not one's goal to report the results of his own research to fellow specialists but rather to address a wider circle of hearers and readers in a way the average person can understand.

My thanks go to my friends Peter Stuhlmacher and Friedrich Mildenberger for their careful examination of the material and their stimulating suggestions, and to my assistant, Klaus W. Müller, for his help in obtaining materials, for his collaboration on the bibliography, for reading through the galleys with me, and, not least, for a great deal of fruitful discussion.

Introduction:
The Problem of Christ and Power

You might be tempted to think my formulation of the topic is imprecise, even misleading. For the question immediately arises, What power does Christ have in our world today? What was the basis for his power back when Christianity began? Does his power have anything in common with "the ruling powers"? Has it anything to do with the power of the state or of money? Or what about the fundamental principle of our scientific-technical culture, which Francis Bacon expressed prophetically with the formula, "Knowledge is power"? Is there any connection with that well-known statement of the most successful revolutionary statesman of our time, "Political power grows out of the barrel of a gun," together with its corollary, "War can only be abolished through war, and in order to get rid of the gun it is necessary to take up the gun"?[1]

Is there a link here with Nietzsche's oft-quoted statement about "the unconditioned will to power, to overpower, with the intention of producing a ruling caste—the future lords of the earth"?[2] That statement is quite close to the first quotation, and yet at the same time it calls our attention to the entirely different statement of Nietzsche's friend Jacob Burckhardt: "Now power is of its nature evil, whoever wields it. It is not stability but a lust, and *ipso facto* insatiable, therefore unhappy in itself and

1. *Quotations from Chairman Mao Tse-Tung* (Peking: Foreign Languages Press, 1966), pp. 61, 63.
2. Friedrich Nietzsche, *The Will to Power*, trans. Anthony M. Ludovici, vol. 2; *The Complete Works of Friedrich Nietzsche*, ed. Oscar Levy (New York: Russell and Russell, 1964), vol. 15, bk. 4.1.4, sec. 957, p. 363.

doomed to make others unhappy."[3]   Here one can easily agree
with Karl Barth's judgment that the prophecies of both Nietzsche
and Burckhardt with regard to the twentieth century have so far
been fulfilled to the letter.[4]

It also seems easy to render a second judgment: Christ cannot
be identified with such "powers."   And this, of course, makes it
all the more difficult to answer the counterquestion, Then what
about the power of the church?   For the New Testament calls the
church "the body of Christ."   What about its actual power, or its
"will to power"?   In the course of their history haven't the
churches become disastrously enmeshed with all those powers
mentioned above?   To hear sociologists and psychologists tell it,
the will to power, that is, the striving to have one's own point of
view prevail, to satisfy one's own desire for authority, to acquire
one's own space to move about freely (thus constricting the freedom of others), is basic to every healthy person, not least the so-
called intellectual.   The feeling of self-worth a person needs in
order to live is closely connected with the possibility of developing his or her will to power in some form and thereby achieving
freedom, at the expense of others if necessary.   In various philosophical and theological encyclopedias one repeatedly runs across
a definition by Max Weber that appears to be fundamental:
" 'Power' [*Macht*] is the probability that one actor within a social
relationship will be in a position to carry out his own will despite
resistance, regardless of the basis on which this probability rests."[5]
If such power is acknowledged and thereby legitimized and
institutionalized, then authority emerges.   In this sense all social
organizations are groups with recognized lines of authority, not
least the churches; that, in fact, is what they were from the beginning.   The earliest Christian community was founded upon the

3. Jacob Burckhardt, *Force and Freedom: Reflections on History,* ed.
James Hastings Nichols (New York: Pantheon Books, 1964), p. 184.

4. Karl Barth, *Church Dogmatics,* trans. and ed. G. W. Bromiley and T. F.
Torrance (Edinburgh: T. and T. Clark, 1961), vol. 3, part 4, sec. 55.1,
p. 391.

5. Max Weber, *Economy and Society,* ed. Günther Roth and Claus Wittich
(New York: Bedminster Press, 1968), vol. 1, sec. 16, p. 53.

experience of the power of the crucified and risen one and upon
the authority—derived therefrom—of the apostles as witnesses of
this resurrection. This raises the question about the forms of this
power and the changes they underwent during the course of time.
Since the topic is so multilayered and complex that it can scarcely
be comprehended, I can select only certain typical features. As a
New Testament scholar I shall concentrate on early Christianity
and, building on this material, I shall also attempt to shed light
briefly on the solution to the problem during the Reformation and
in contemporary theology. And even though I shall not completely lose sight of the question of power structures within the
church, the emphasis will have to be on the conflict of Christ and
his church with the political powers.

1

Concerning the History-of-Religions Problem of Power

Power is a fundamental religious phenomenon, a primal experience of prehistorical humanity which very likely belongs to the constitutive foundations of what it means to be human. Primitive people experienced the different, the extraordinary, the superhuman—threatening or pleasant—as numinous power. This is true of the confrontation with forces of nature as well as with other people. Even the particularly successful person, whether warrior, hunter, or medicine man, is a power-bearer and possesses, therefore, a numinous authority. This power is beyond good and evil; it is ethically neutral and encompasses black magic *and* cures, blessing *and* curse. People's reaction to the phenomenon of power is "amazement [*Scheu*], and in extreme cases fear; . . . objects and persons endowed with this potency have that essential nature of their own which we call 'sacred.'"[1]

In nature religions the gods become bearers of this kind of concentrated power. The Greek pantheon serves as a vivid example. Aphrodite embraces the powers of love and feminine beauty, Ares the horrors of war, Dionysus drunkenness and festive joy, Apollo prophecy and music, and, at the same time, the powers of sickness and death—he is both destroyer and savior. Over the entire family of gods stands Zeus as true patriarch, "the father of gods and humans," the god of heaven, the ruler of fate and guardian of the right.

We do not wish to tarry over these well-known figures. What interests us is the end of Greek nature religion in the Hellenistic

1. Gerardus van der Leeuw, *Religion in Essence and Manifestation: A Study in Phenomenology*, trans. J. E. Turner (London: Allen and Unwin, 1938), p. 28.

enlightenment, in which the ancient faith of the ancestors crumbles. Here the gods are reduced to symbols: Aphrodite for sexuality, Dionysus for wine and drunkenness. Zeus himself becomes the cipher for inexplicable destiny; the Stoics identify him with Heimarmene, or Fate. It is, of course, Tyche (called Fortuna by the Romans), deceptive fortune or blind chance, who becomes the actual, ruling, almighty divinity. Therefore she is often portrayed with a blindfold. "Fortune rules everything," says a popular proverb. According to Pliny the Elder, "all over the world, in all places, and at all times, Fortune is the only god whom every one invokes; she alone is spoken of, she alone is accused and is supposed to be guilty . . ."[2]

2. *The Natural History of Pliny* 2.5, trans. John Bostock and H. T. Riley (London: Henry G. Bohn, 1855), vol. 1, p. 23.

2
Concerning
Political Religion in Antiquity

The other wielder of power, which achieves divine honor in that time of enlightenment, is humanity itself. While the ancient gods were being portrayed in human form and demoted to great rulers of primeval times, the contemporary wielders of power were accorded superhuman, divine honors in the *political pseudoreligion of the ruler-cult.* This becomes clearly visible for the first time in that colossal figure Alexander the Great. During his famous visit to the oracle of the god Amon in the oasis at Siwah, the priest is supposed to have whispered that he was "the Son of Zeus," that God himself had appointed him ruler of the world.[1] This new, totally *political* religion of the time of enlightenment was motivated not only by reasons of state but also by a genuine necessity. This is shown by the hymn the Athenians sang to the glory of the brilliant playboy and adventurer Demetrius Poliorcetes at his entry into the city in 291 B.C.:

> O offspring of the mightiest of gods, Poseidon, and of Aphrodite,
> hail!
> The other gods are either far away or have no ears,
> Or are not, or pay no slightest heed to us; but thee we see face to
> face,
> Not in wood and not in stone, but verily and in truth!
> And so we pray to thee:
> First bring us peace, thou dearest (of the gods)! For thou art
> Lord [i.e., it is within thy power].[2]

1. Diodorus Siculus, *Bibliotheca historica* 17.51; Plutarch, *Alexander* 27.4–5.
2. Duris of Samos, quoted in Athenaeus, *Deipnosophists* 6.63.253 d–f; cited from Frederick C. Grant, ed., *Hellenistic Religions* (Indianapolis, Ind.: Bobbs-Merrill, 1953), p. 67.

The Hellenistic kings of the Diadochian period and the later Roman emperors, whose legitimation depended first and foremost on the possession of absolute power in the state, saw in the variable forms of the new cult a favorable opportunity to establish their constantly threatened authority metaphysically. The Greek concept of God, in keeping with the anonymous character of power in nature religions, was not bound to a personal encounter, but merely gave expression in statement form to one's confrontation with superhuman, supernatural powers. Thus it was not difficult to interpret the absolute power of the king (*basileus*) or prince (*princeps*) as a divine dominion transcending that of an ordinary human being. This was especially true if the ruler proclaimed his benevolence and allowed himself to be extolled as the savior and benefactor of his subjects.

Augustus is the best example. Completing the work of his adoptive father and great-uncle, Julius Caesar, he ended the civil war and stabilized the empire. Soon after Caesar's murder he gave himself the title *divi filius,* "son of the deified one." The Greek East, accustomed to the ruler-cult, accordingly named him "Son of God" (*theou huios*); a Greek inscription from Egypt naturally made of this a "God born of God" (*theos ek theou*).[3] The divine ruler became redeemer as well. In 17 B. C., after the horrors of a civil war lasting almost a hundred years, he proclaimed a century of peace. The time of salvation, the Golden Age, appeared to be dawning. The Pax Romana established by Augustus became from then on an essential component of the imperial religious ideology about the state.

A preliminary form of the emperor cult, which attached itself seamlessly to the Hellenistic cult of the kings, was the cult of the goddess Roma in the Greek-speaking East. She symbolized the irresistible force of Roman imperialism. In this way the state and

3. *Orientis Graeci Inscriptiones Selectae,* ed. Wilhelm Dittenberger (Leipzig: Hirzel, 1905), vol. 2, no. 655 (24 B.C.), p. 365; cf. Fritz Taeger, *Charisma. Studien zur Geschichte des antiken Herrscherkultes* (Stuttgart: Kohlhammer, 1960), vol. 2, p. 98.

its representatives became metaphysically exalted and claimed to embody the revelation of divine power. The ruler-cult and the traditional belief in Rome's divine mission fused into an inseparable unity. According to Virgil's *Aeneid* Jupiter promised, "To Romans I set no boundary in space or time; I have granted them dominion, and it has no end."[4] Possessing such power Rome becomes, as it were, the God-appointed teacher of the human race: "But you, Roman, must remember that you have to guide the nations by your authority, for this is to be your skill, to teach the ways of peace, to show mercy to the conquered, and to wage war until the haughty are brought low."[5]

Correspondingly Horace designates Augustus the almighty Prince of Peace:

> While Caesar stands guard, peace is assured, the peace
> No power can break—not civil dissension or
> Brute force or wrath, that weapon forger,
> Misery-maker for warring cities.[6]

There was virtually no opposition to this "imperial metaphysics," with *one* exception—that tiny nation of Jews and the community of Christians that emerged therefrom. Antiochus IV, who called himself Epiphanes (the Manifest [God]), tried as early as 167 B. C., with the help of radical Jewish apostates, to eradicate the Jewish religion and to turn the temple into a shrine for Zeus. The megalomaniac emperor Caligula, following in his footsteps, wanted in 39 A. D. to set up a statue of himself (depicted as Jupiter) in the temple of Jerusalem, since the Jews refused to accord him the worship that was his due. Only through his assassination was a general rebellion by the Jews averted. Hadrian finished the job, giving the command in 132 A. D. to erect a shrine for Jupiter Capitolinus on the ruins of the destroyed

4. Virgil, *The Aeneid* 1.278–79, trans. W. F. Jackson Knight (Baltimore: Penguin, 1966), p. 36; cf. Antonie Wlosok, *Rom und die Christen* (Stuttgart: Klett, 1970), p. 65.

5. Ibid. 6.851 ff., p. 173 (translation altered).

6. *The Odes of Horace* 4.15, trans. James Michie (New York: Washington Square Press, 1965), p. 251.

temple, thereby touching off the desperate final revolt of the Jews under Bar Kokhba. This time Rome remained the (apparent) victor.

Enlightened demythologizing of the Greek pantheon thus reduced the divine powers to "the force of destiny"—a formulation that has behind it more than just the title of Verdi's opera; but at the same time there was a deification of human political power. That both, apparently opposite, conceptions could combine is illustrated by the show of reverence for the "fortune" or the "genius" of the emperor by means of the oath that played a decisive role in the trials of Christians. It is understandable that in response to this demand for allegiance Origen could designate "the fortune of the emperor" as a wicked demon who brings evil upon the emperor.[7] When one makes human power divine one really unleashes the demons!

7. Origen, *Contra Celsum*, 8.65.

3
Theocracy
and Ancient Judaism

In its appeal to the power of God ancient Israel not only contested the potency of the non-Israelite gods (disdainfully calling them "trifles, devoid of reality"), but also *critically turned against every self-glorifying display of human power*:

> A king does not win because of his powerful army;
>   a soldier does not triumph because of his strength.
> War horses are useless for victory;
>   their great strength cannot save.
> The Lord watches over those who fear him,
>   those who trust his constant love. [Ps. 33:16–18, TEV; cf. Pss.
>   20:8; 147:10–11, Prov. 21:31]

Jahweh's word, spoken through Isaiah, against Israel's alliances with other powers makes the same point: "In returning and rest you shall be saved, in quietness and in trust shall be your strength" (Isa. 30:15). Zerubbabel, who during the reign of the Persian king Darius awaited the full restoration of the Davidic kingdom, and who himself was seen as the one to be designated Messiah, receives the directive through the prophet Zechariah: "Not by might, nor by power, but by my Spirit, says the Lord of hosts" (Zech 4:6). On this basis all presumptuous claims of divinity made by an oriental king had to be rejected sharply. This is shown by the song of ridicule occasioned by the fall of the king of Babylon:

> How you are fallen from heaven,
>   O Day Star, son of Dawn!
> How you are cut down to the ground,
>   you who laid the nations low!
> You said in your heart,

"I will ascend to heaven;
above the stars of God
   I will set my throne on high;
. . . .
I will ascend above the heights of the clouds,
   I will make myself like the Most High."
But you are brought down to Sheol,
   to the depths of the Pit.
Those who see you will stare at you,
   and ponder over you:
"Is this the man who made the earth tremble,
   who shook kingdoms,
who made the world like a desert . . . ?" [Isa. 14:12–17]

Against such a background it is understandable that a confrontation was unavoidable between Old Testament Jewish faith in the one God and Lord of history and Hellenistic-Roman "political religion." The literary expression of this confrontation survives in the so-called apocalypse, a genre typical of the thinking of broad circles of Palestinian Judaism.

The earliest apocalyptic book is Daniel, written in the Maccabean period (165 B. C.). In this book the conflict finds a classical expression that was to exert an extraordinarily strong influence as time went on. The philosophy of history that would emerge in the West found its source here. The course of history is determined by four successive world powers, whose godless hubris reaches its climax in the last of the four, Macedonia and Greece. It culminates in the persecution of God's people and the desecration of the sanctuary. At a predetermined time, in the midst of woes beyond measure, the shameless enemy of God is to be annihilated by a divine miracle, God's kingdom (and thus Israel's dominion) inaugurated, and the course of history ended.

With numerous variations this theocratic-apocalyptic ideal shaped the thought and action of great masses of the population in Jewish Palestine for the next three hundred years, right up to the catastrophic rebellion under Bar Kokhba in 132–135 A. D. Some, following Daniel and the ancient prophets, expected the end to come solely through God's direct, miraculous intervention.

Others, on the other hand, dreamt of their own action and the "holy war" led by the Messiah. Precisely in Jesus' time radical groups inaugurated the end-time war of liberation in the form of revolutionary guerrilla warfare and took the logical view that any loyalty to the Roman emperor-god was an idolatrous breaking of the first commandment, since God, the Lord and King of Israel, had sole claim to the titles of Lord (*kyrios*) and King (*basileus*). Thus the notion of freedom (*cherût*) appears as a political counterpart to the traditional concept of the reign of God. It appears for the first time on coins minted in the Jewish rebellions of 66–70 and 132–35 A. D. A little later we find it in the tenth petition of the Eighteen Benedictions, the principal Jewish prayer, edited shortly after 70 A. D.: "Sound the great horn *for our freedom*; raise the ensign to gather our exiles, and gather us from the four corners of the earth. Blessed art thou, O Lord, who gatherest the dispersed of thy people Israel."[1]

What actually happened was, of course, totally different. The result of these desperately bitter wars of liberation was not the establishment of the messianic kingdom but the destruction of the second temple by Titus in 70 A. D. and the extermination of Jewry in Egypt, Cyrenaica, and on Cyprus in 116–117 A. D., as well as in its center, Judea, about 65 years after the destruction of the temple as a consequence of the rebellion under the pseudo-Messiah Bar Kokhba in 132–135 A. D. For the Jews, this was the start of an eighteen-hundred-year history of political powerlessness and persecution as a religious and political minority, a history during which, it is true, they gave extraordinary proof of the power of their faith in the God of their fathers.

1. Joseph H. Hertz, ed., *The Authorized Daily Prayer Book*, rev. ed. (New York: Bloch, 1963), p. 143 (italics mine).

4
Jesus of Nazareth and the Powers of His Time

It is in this highly charged atmosphere that we have to picture Jesus' activity. It has nothing, absolutely nothing at all to do with the Nazarene idyll which falsified the portrait of Jesus in recent centuries and which, strange to say, we encounter again today in idealized portraits of revolutionary leaders. He was executed as an alleged political criminal, on a cross, as were several thousand Jews in that century; sentenced to death and executed by the Roman authorities, to whom he was handed over by the Sadducean leaders of the people. He was despised by the law-observant and the zealous, forsaken even by his disciples.

We cannot provide here a sketch of Jesus' proclamation and work. Only two of its components interest us, though these are certainly fundamental: (1) his relationship to the political powers, whether to the foreign oppressors and the upper class that was in league with them or to the theocratic and nationalistic power of the Jewish liberation movement; and (2) the secret of his influence, the charismatic power by which, although he appeared for a very short time in a small, out-of-the-way region of the world, he changed the world as no other person has.

People have wanted to see him as a political revolutionary as well as an apolitical fanatic, indeed even as an agent of the occupation forces. Those kinds of tendentious misinterpretations refute themselves. One could put as a heading over his entire work the passage from Zechariah we quoted above: "Not by might, nor by power, but by my Spirit, says the Lord of hosts." *The Spirit of God* manifested itself in Jesus' outwardly simple style of preaching, whose effectiveness lay solely in the content of his

message, and in his deeds of kindness. Basically Jesus' work was
set out beforehand through the prophetic word of Trito-Isaiah:

> The Spirit of the Lord God is upon me,
>   because the Lord has anointed me
> to bring good tidings to the afflicted;
>   he has sent me to bind up the brokenhearted,
> to proclaim liberty to the captives,
>   and the opening of the prison to those who are bound;
> to proclaim the year of the Lord's favor,
>   and the day of vengeance of our God;
>   to comfort all who mourn;
> to grant to those who mourn in Zion—
>   to give them a garland instead of a faint spirit;
> that they may be called oaks of righteousness,
>   the planting of the Lord, that he may be glorified.
>
> [Isa. 61:1–3]

Luke puts the beginning of the passage on Jesus' lips during
his inaugural sermon in Nazareth (Luke 4:18 ff.). This passage
also influences the beatitudes, in which the "powerless" are promised salvation (6:20). It shapes Jesus' answer to John the Baptist
(7:22) and gives appropriate expression to Jesus' proclamation
about God's liberating love for all the lost and lowly, a proclamation that is not restricted to the preached word but also includes
his actions, for example, his table fellowship with tax gatherers
and sinners and his charismatic healings.

The concept that is the key to his message is the *reign of God*.
This concept comes from prophetic-apocalyptic sources, yet attains an entirely new form with Jesus: this reign is about to break
in; indeed in his activity it is in a hidden way already present. It
becomes identical with the Father's overwhelming love for all the
outcasts and the despised—one need only think of the unique
parable about the prodigal son—and yet it also entails judgment
on the self-righteous and the unmerciful. Since God alone is
judge, people need no longer fight for their own rights, or despise
and condemn their neighbors (Matt. 7:1 ff.). Even more, all
nationalistic and theocratic tendencies disappear in Jesus' preaching. There is no talk either about the annihilation of the ungodly
world power or about the coming rule by Israel. On the contrary,

Gentiles and Samaritans are held before the impenitent people of God as examples of true repentance and love.

Jesus' activity must have appeared reactionary to the revolutionary Zealots; to the leaders of the people in their subservience to Rome, on the other hand, it must have appeared politically dangerous. For he had considerable influence on the humble Galilean peasants, and people correctly perceived behind his appearance a messianic claim. But a person with a claim on the title Messiah was seen, for that very reason, as a threat to the power of the Romans and their Jewish accomplices. It was thus not difficult for these accomplices, by denouncing him as a messianic pretender, to force Pilate to condemn the accused. Charged with wanting to be "King of the Jews," he died on the cross as a political criminal and revolutionary.

That Jesus met such an end must appear logical *in view of the critical light he shed on the ruling powers among his people.* He set himself against the rich landowners of the feudal upper class, for example, when he characterized as idolatry an attachment to "unrighteous mammon": "No one can serve two masters. . . . You cannot serve God and mammon" (Matt. 6:24). Therefore the rich man has forfeited his part in the kingdom of God; only a miracle of God can save him (Mark 10:25; Luke 16:19 ff.). The Torah of Moses and its guardians and stewards, the Pharisaic scribes, fall short of fulfilling the Father's perfect will, which becomes fully manifest in the radical and unrestricted love command. All individual laws of the Torah about the Sabbath, temple service, and so on, are to be subordinated to this command; indeed as particular words of Jesus about divorce, swearing, or uncleanliness show, these individual laws are in part abrogated. Jesus thus makes a direct attack on the center of the Jewish theocracy's power, the Torah, and it is understandable that the Pharisaic scribes, spiritual leaders of the majority of the Jewish people, saw in Jesus' activity a deadly threat. Since God's reign is breaking in, the original benevolent will of the Father in heaven must be put into practice in ways that in certain circumstances run counter to the letter of the Torah of Moses.

Jesus levels a further attack at the power of the priestly Sadducean hierarchy in the temple. The so-called cleansing of the
temple was certainly no act of revolutionary violence aimed, let
us say, at occupying the sanctuary, but merely a provocative
symbolic action of the kind that is already present in the Old
Testament with Jeremiah. In such cases the conspicuous action
causes offense, but it is the accompanying prophetic word of
reproach that is decisive: ". . . but you have made it a den of
thieves" (Mark 11:17; cf. Jer. 7:11). By this demonstration Jesus
probably wanted to denounce the monopoly in monetary ex-
change and trade enjoyed by the high-priestly families in the
temple. It seems likely that this protest action hastened the decision by the leaders of the people to have Jesus put to death. Thus
one cannot conclude on the basis of this turbulent scene that Jesus
justified the use of physical force. He waged his battle with the
ruling powers of his people—to use a formulation in the Augsburg
Confession—*sine vi humana, sed verbo,* "without human power,
simply by the word."[1] This is confirmed by his end, which he
consciously faced and did not evade. For who could have
stopped him or his disciples from joining the freedom fighters in
the Judean wilderness?

At the Last Supper Jesus imparted to his disciples the benefits
of his death. Then, in Gethsemane, came his final wrestling with
God for certainty about his way of suffering. His word to the
unnamed disciple at his arrest, "Put your sword back in its
sheath," as well as the accompanying statement about the more
than twelve legions of angels his father could send—words which
Matthew ascribes to him (26:52–53)—are, to be sure, later elabo-
rations, but they are fundamentally correct reproductions of Jesus'
intention to renounce force. It is consistent with this that he
could heighten the love command to its ultimate, and to this day
its most offensive conclusion, love for one's enemy, and could
make the paradoxical demand to renounce all physical resistance
(Matt. 5:38–48). For him true freedom is freedom from the
compulsion to assert oneself at all costs. It appears likely to me

1. Augsburg Confession 28.21, *The Book of Concord,* trans. and ed.
Theodore G. Tappert (Philadelphia: Fortress, 1959), p. 84.

that this demand was formulated with direct reference to the theocratic and nationalistic liberation movement in which hatred toward an enemy was regarded as a good work. The overwhelming, disarming power of Jesus' message—then as well as now—lies not least in this fundamental renunciation of external means of exerting power. A necessary consequence is willingness to surrender one's own life for Jesus' cause: "For whoever would save his life will lose it; and whoever loses his life for my sake and the gospel's will save it" (Mark 8:35).

In view of the sharp conflict Jesus had with the ruling groups among his own people, the question arises whether he had a similar negative estimate of the power of the Roman government. Our sources are silent on that point. That he was critical of the ruler of his own territory, Herod Antipas, who permitted the murder of John the Baptist, is shown by his answer to Pharisees who warned him of Herod's attempts to kill him: "Go and tell that fox, . . . 'I must go on my way today and tomorrow and the day following; for it cannot be that a prophet should perish away from Jerusalem'" (Luke 13:32–33). That is to say, he reckoned with his own violent death in the Holy City, but not at the hands of the tetrarch Herod. His other, oft-quoted word, "Render to Caesar the things that are Caesar's, and to God the things that are God's" (Mark 12:27), no one can dare misunderstand as a stance of loyal submission to the state. First of all, Jesus utters this word in a threatening conflict situation. His opponents want, after all, to base a political accusation on his answer—no matter what it turns out to be. Secondly, the whole emphasis lies on the second half of the sentence; the *and* is to be understood adversatively and rendered *but*. The decisive issue is not, as the Zealots thought, the refusal to pay taxes, but rather absolute obedience to the will of God. Whoever has in his possession the emperor's coins should without further ado give them back to their owner, that is, pay his taxes. The only thing that really matters is obedience to God's command. The nearness of the reign of God relativizes even the power of Rome. The political religion of the all-powerful empire is—in total contrast to the Zealot protest—pushed aside as devoid of power; indeed it is not even taken into account. By the power of his word Jesus battles to have his people really acknowledge God's will. But their hatred for the foreign oppressors only establishes their own self-righteousness.

A fundamentally critical stance over against all political powers becomes clear in Jesus' instruction to his disciples as they, in a very human way, fought over who should be considered greatest. Luke offers this word as Jesus' farewell discourse, at the conclusion of the Last Supper: "The kings of the Gentiles exercise lordship over them; and those in authority over them are called benefactors. But not so with you; rather let the greatest among you become as the youngest, and the leader as one who serves. . . . I am among you as one who serves" (Luke 22:25–27; cf. Mark 10:42–45).

In the same context in John's gospel we have the account of the foot-washing (13:4–14). In contrast to those who wield political power, the true authority of the disciple lies in his renunciation of status and power and in his readiness to serve. That is to say, for those who follow Jesus there is *freedom from domination*. The early church reformulated this word and applied it to Jesus' death: "For the Son of man also came not to be served but to serve, and to give his life as a ransom for many" (Mark 10:45). Jesus' primary service is his self-sacrifice; in the ultimate renunciation of power, the way of salvation is opened for all people.

In what has been said to this point, the secret of Jesus' immense effect on the simple people in Galilee has already been alluded to repeatedly. In the gospels it is described through the concept of charismatic authority (*exousia*). Here is how Matthew summarizes the impact of Jesus' proclamation at the conclusion of the Sermon on the Mount: "And when Jesus finished these sayings, the crowds were astonished at his teaching, for he taught them as one who had authority, and not as their scribes" (Matt. 7:28–29, in dependence on Mark 1:22, 27).

It is all the more striking that in the examples we have of Jesus' preaching there is an absence of provocative and demagogic tendencies. In fact, even in Greek translation the polished, poetic form of his sayings and maxims shines through. In using pictures and parables it was not his intention to conceal in an esoteric, apocalyptic manner but above all, by rational argument alone, to explain and clarify, that is, to reach an *understanding* with the hearer. Through the charismatic authority of his word Jesus did not seek to seduce his hearer in an irrational manner but to convince, to gain free assent. The "reign of God," the "nearness of God's love," challenged the hearer to a clear decision. It aimed at genuine repentance by the individual, which at the same time meant that it opposed repressive group pressure.

Beside Jesus' powerfully effective word stands the authority of what he did. He practices table fellowship with the outcasts, the despised and the ungodly, the pariahs of Jewish society, and dares to announce that God accepts them. Indeed, he himself forgives sin by messianic "authority" (Mark 2:5), calls unlikely people as disciples in the service of God's reign, similar to the way God himself called prophets in the Old Testament. He heals sick people whom no one else would have helped, thereby fulfilling the prophetic promise for the messianic age (Matt. 11:5; cf. Isa. 29:18–19; 35:5–6; 61:1 ff.). He understands the healings and exorcisms as an end-time victory over the powers of evil (Luke 11:20; cf. 10:18). His messianic mission, to announce the true and ultimate will of God by word and deed, lifts him above Moses, the bringer of the Torah, and the prophets of the old covenant: "You have heard that it was said to our ancestors . . . But I say unto you . . ." (Matt. 5:21; cf. vss. 27, 33). "Behold, something greater than Solomon is here. . . . behold, something greater than Jonah is here" (Luke 11:31–32). Ernst Fuchs is right when he describes Jesus' unique messianic authority by saying that "he dares to act in God's stead,"[2] that he not only proclaims God's love to the lost but puts it into effect by what he does. Jesus' renunciation of force, his trust in the unencumbered word, is an essential element of his activity "in God's stead."

---

2. Ernst Fuchs, *Zur Frage nach dem historischen Jesus. Gesammelte Aufsätze* (Tübingen: J. C. B. Mohr, 1960), vol. 2, p. 156.

5
Power and
Powerlessness in the Early Church

When Jesus was executed the disciples experienced total powerlessness and humiliating failure. Their master had failed under
the gaze of the entire nation; they themselves had forsaken and
denied him. According to the Torah he was accursed, since he
had been crucified (Deut. 21:23).

The appearances of the risen one created out of Jesus' inco-
hesive band of followers an authentic new community, the church.
At the same time this unexpected event, overturning all human
conceptions, unleashed a chain of consequences: the new congregation understood itself as the true people of God for the end-
time, who awaited the return of their Lord, exalted at God's right
hand, as the coming Son of man/Messiah. They knew themselves to be in possession of the newly outpoured prophetic
Spirit, and they obeyed the call of the risen one to summon his
own apostate people to repentence.

*The early Christian mission is a direct consequence of the
resurrection event.* Jesus, the crucified preacher of the reign of
God, now became the content of the new missionary proclamation as the messianic perfecter of that reign and as the one whom
God empowered to be the judge. Reflection on the form and
origin of the new message of salvation was the starting point for
early Christian theology, which unfolded in a remarkable way
about twenty years later in the letters of the apostle Paul. This
new message, like the message of Jesus, was borne along solely
through the power of the word and the helping deed which
accompanied it.

According to the introduction of Paul's Romans letter, the gospel he is proclaiming is "the power of God [*dynamis theou*] for salvation to everyone who has faith" (Rom. 1:16). At the beginning of 1 Corinthians he says it with even more precision: "For the word of the cross is folly to those who are perishing, but to us who are being saved it is the power of God" (1:18). A little later he says that his preaching, which led to the establishment of the congregation in that port city, came "in demonstration of the Spirit and of power" (2:4). (About seventeen hundred years later Lessing—to no avail—demanded this demonstration from the Lutheran Church of his time.) When Paul wrote to Corinth, about twenty-five years after Christianity's founding, the Christian community was an obscure sect within the despised Jewish religious and national community. What set the Christian community apart was only its fanatical missionary zeal, its despising of the world, which offended the educated, and the fact that it no longer took the Jewish law so seriously, which led even "superstitious non-Jews" to flock to it. Members of the establishment avoided this new sect with a passion: "For consider your call, brethren; not many of you were wise according to worldly standards, not many were powerful, not many were of noble birth . . ." (1 Cor. 1:26).

In addition to those in Syria, Christian communities existed in several larger cities in Asia Minor and Greece and, not least, even in Rome, where, according to the famous report about Christians in the *Annals* of Tacitus, "all things hideous and shameful from every part of the world find their centre and become popular."[1] They were a tiny minority, whose insignificance stood at first in inverse proportion to their claim of universal salvation. Nero, in brutally persecuting them about eight or nine years later as scapegoats for the burning of Rome, may have been influenced partially by his wife, Poppaea Sabina. But the principal reason probably was that this "mischievous superstition" (*exitabilis superstitio*), against which the blanket reproach was levelled of *odium humani*

---

1. Tacitus, *Annals* 15.44, in *The Complete Works of Tacitus*, trans. A. J. Church and W. J. Brodribb, and ed. Moses Hadas (New York: Modern Library, 1942), pp. 380–81.

generis, that is, "hatred against mankind," found only despisers and no advocates. Tacitus, it is true, condemns the inhuman cruelty with which the Christians were tortured during the Neronian persecution, but at the same time he clearly expresses his infinitely deep contempt for this new, peculiar sect. It was in the physician Galen (129–199 A. D.) that the Christians found for the first time a more understanding critic, who was not silent about his admiration for their "philosophical" way of life, even though he felt obliged to find fault with their credulity.

In all likelihood there is scarcely a group in the history of the world which, relying totally on the word entrusted to it, embodied a greater discrepancy between outward powerlessness and inner, victorious certainty of power than the primitive Christian community. At the conclusion of Romans 8, the letter's central chapter, Paul sketches this tension, which a historical observer finds almost incomprehensible:

> If God is for us, who is against us? He who did not spare his own Son but gave him up for us all, will he not also give us all things with him? Who shall bring any charge against God's elect? It is God who justifies; who is to condemn? Is it Christ Jesus, who died, yes, who was raised from the dead, who is at the right hand of God, who indeed intercedes for us? Who shall separate us from the love of Christ? Shall tribulation, or distress, or persecution, or famine, or nakedness, or peril, or sword? As it is written, "For thy sake we are being killed all the day long; we are regarded as sheep to be slaughtered" [Ps. 44:22]. No, in all these things we are more than conquerors through him who loved us. For I am sure that neither death, nor life, nor angels, nor principalities, nor things present, nor things to come . . . nor anything else in all creation, will be able to separate us from the love of God in Christ Jesus our Lord. [Rom. 8:31–39]

One could characterize this confession as a classical description of that *dynamis* (power) of the gospel about which the apostle speaks at the beginning of his letter. At the same time he sets before the eyes of a perplexed twentieth-century Christendom what the word *faith* means. The christological center is decisive: since God himself, in Jesus of Nazareth, threw in his lot with the ultimate powerlessness of human existence, he permits the be-

liever to participate in his world-conquering power, which mani-
fests itself in faith, love, and hope.

The ancient Christ-hymn in Philippians 2:6–11 gives classical
expression to this *emptying of the son of God*:

> His state was divine,
> yet he did not cling
> to his equality with God
> but emptied himself
> to assume the condition of a slave,
> and became as men are;
> and being as all men are,
> he was humbler yet,
> even to accepting death,
> death on a cross.
> But God raised him high
> and gave him the name
> which is above all other names
> so that *all beings*
> in the heavens, on earth and in the underworld,
> *should bend the knee* at the name of Jesus
> and that every tongue should acclaim
> Jesus Christ as Lord,
> to the glory of God the Father.
>
> [Jerusalem Bible]

It is one of the greatest enigmas of early Christian history, and
at the same time a testimony to the strict consistency of the primitive community's theological thinking, that the primal event of
Jesus' activity, the event that founded the community, namely,
his death and resurrection appearances, very quickly developed
into a christology that extends back to divine pre-existence, sees
the son of God as a participant in the creation and the revelation
of the old covenant (1 Cor. 8:6; Col. 1:15 ff.; 1 Cor. 10:4), and
yet expresses his essential nature in his being sent into the world
and in his ultimate self-emptying in the passion. Christ's volun-
tary sacrifice and powerlessness lay the foundation for his work
of salvation as well as his end-time power as God's plenipotentiary.

Reconciliation is a key concept for Paul as he describes the
work of salvation. It is through reconciliation that humanity,

alienated from its origin and destiny, finds its way back to its essential nature as God's creature and becomes a "new creation" (2 Cor. 5:17; cf. Rom. 5:10). The apostle sees in the gospel the "power to produce change," and this frees him from all autocratic and law-centered forces, frees him for a new life, in which "the fruit of the Spirit"—"love, joy, peace, patience . . ." (Gal. 5:22)— takes over. This "power to produce change" was at work in Paul's own case in that he, the Pharisee and persecutor of Christians, was entrusted, through his vision of Christ near Damascus, with "the ministry of reconciliation" (2 Cor. 5:18) as an ambassador for Christ. It further shows itself in the overcoming of barriers that were especially grievous in the ancient world, those of nation and class: in Christ's community "there is neither Jew nor Greek, there is neither slave nor free, there is neither male nor female; for you are all one in Christ Jesus" (Gal. 3:28; cf. Col. 3:11).

Even though the community knows that "all power both in heaven and on earth has been given" (Matt. 28:18) to the risen one as God's "representative," and that all heavenly and earthly "powers" must bow the knee before him (Phil. 2:10–11), it nevertheless participates in such power only *by serving.*

This happens in the Spirit-empowered proclamation of the word, in the loving deed—Paul speaks of "faith working through love" (Gal. 5:6)—and, not least, in *suffering in imitation of Christ*:

> For it seems to me God has made us apostles the most abject of mankind. We are like men condemned to death in the arena, a spectacle to the whole universe—angels, as well as men. We are fools for Christ's sake. . . . To this day we go hungry and thirsty and in rags; we are roughly handled; we wander from place to place; we wear ourselves out working with our own hands. They curse us, and we bless; they persecute us, and we submit to it; they slander us, and we humbly make our appeal. We are treated as the scum of the earth, the dregs of humanity, to this very day. [1 Cor. 4:9–13, NEB]

These last sentences agree remarkably with the oldest appraisal of early Christianity by heathen writers such as Tacitus, Suetonius, Pliny, Fronto, Lucian, and Celsus. Only when forced into it by his Corinthian opponents, and totally against his will, does Paul make reference to revelations he had received from the Lord. This same Lord denied his request for relief from a severe illness: "My grace is all you need; power comes to its full strength in weakness." The apostle confirms this by adding, "for when I am weak, then I am strong" (2 Cor. 12:9–10, NEB). For this very reason the primitive community's apostolic message can never serve as the basis for a "theology of glory" but rather only for a "theology of the cross." The actual way of the community in this world has been traced out by the earthly, the crucified Christ, and not by the risen Christ in his glory. This risen Christ is not at our beck and call; he cannot be seen. Our only access to him is through a hope that has nothing to cling to except Jesus' own promise. The conquest over the powers of evil promised the community happens only in the context of faith that in obedience to God lives from the word of the gospel (Rom. 10:6–17). Christ's victory over death as the "last enemy" (1 Cor. 15:26) is certain only for faith living by hope, faith that boldly disregards the all-too-powerful reality of our experience.

As is every human organization, the primitive church was faced with problems of organizing and regulating itself appropriately. Accordingly it took some steps toward becoming an "organization with recognized lines of authority." That is, the church also was subject to sociological rules of group formation. To be sure, our sources don't tell us all that much about the earliest period. We are best informed about the Pauline congregations between 50 and 60 A. D. and the Johannine circle about 100 A. D. Luke's sketch of the primitive community in Acts comes close to being an idealized picture that he has projected into the past.

In any case it can be said that the old controversy between Rudolf Sohm and Karl Holl over whether there was from the beginning an official order in the primitive church, together with corresponding forms of governance, or whether the early community knew only free charismatic authority, presents one of those false alternatives that in the field of theology are always fought over with particular vehemence. Through a careful analysis of the earliest report about witnesses to the resurrection (1 Cor. 15:3–9), Karl Holl came to this conclusion—astounding for a Protestant:

> We find in the Christian community from its inception a regular hierarchy, an order established by God, a divine canon law, the church as an institution into which individuals are incorporated. A rigidly delimited group, the "apostles"—that is, James and the Twelve—possesses permanent divine priority attainable by no one else and is thereby empowered to lead the community.[2]

Even though current research no longer agrees with this formulation in all particulars—the identification of the Twelve with the apostles is questionable, for example—one can hardly doubt that the appearances of the risen one in an unrepeatable way established in the community a group whose authority had the "character of law."

Obviously this is just one side of the argument. The free charismatic authority of the word was no less potent. Therefore in Antioch the outsider Paul can oppose Peter, one of the three "pillars" in Jerusalem, with all severity, and point him back to the unalterable truth of the gospel (Gal. 2:11 ff.). Fellowship within the young church was not destroyed over these issues, even if they led to great tensions, as this one basic example may suffice to show. And then even the worship service in the Pauline congregations, which presumably goes back to the worship of older mission congregations in Syria, took shape under the free charism of the prophetic Spirit, each member of the congregation making a contribution in accordance with his or her gift (1 Cor. 12, 14). Nowhere did a congregational leader come forward to determine what happened. The only clear authority was that of the apostle himself. It rested upon his vision of the risen one and on the gospel which the Lord himself entrusted to him (Gal. 1:11 ff.; 1 Cor. 9:1 ff., 15:7 ff.).

2. Karl Holl, "Der Kirchenbegriff des Paulus in seinem Verhältnis zu dem der Urgemeinde," in *Gesammelte Aufsätze zur Kirchengeschichte*, vol. 2, *Der Osten* (Tübingen: J. C. B. Mohr, 1928), p. 54.

It is not until a generation later that the beginnings of an institutionalized "office" become visible in the congregations. Even power struggles do not fail to appear. Thus 1 Clement, dominated by the judicial and order-oriented thinking of the church in Rome, speaks against the deposing of older presbyters by young members of the congregation in Corinth. In addition to pointing to Old Testament examples meant to deter such behavior, the letter also refers—and here a new spirit is visible—to the discipline of the Roman army.[3] While 1 Peter, which arose at the same time as 1 Clement, addresses the totality of the community as the "royal priesthood," and thereby entrusts it with the task of proclaiming the Redeemer's praise (2:9), we find in the Pastoral Epistles, which were written at the beginning of the second century, the initial steps toward an "apostolic succession" in which the "gift for an office" is conferred through the sacramental action of the laying on of hands (2 Tim. 1:6; 1 Tim. 4:14, 5:22).

The monarchical episcopate does not emerge until the second century. The earliest evidence is found in the letters of the martyr Ignatius of Antioch from around 116 A. D. The battle against Gnostic and Montanist heresies, growing pressure from the state, as well as developments in the church's worship, encouraged its establishment. It is significant that already in Ignatius the "administration of the sacraments" and the direction of worship are firmly tied to the person of the bishop. Monarchical episcopate and sacramentalization of ecclesiastical practice go hand in hand. A new element here is the argument for *one* bishop as head of the community. Ignatius repeatedly makes the analogy between the *one* bishop and the *one* God, while he frequently compares the multiplicity of presbyters under him with the apostolic band (Magnesians 6:1; Trallians 3:1; cf. Philadelphians 8:1). What appears here is a philosophical concept which in the "political theology" of late antiquity establishes the absolute power of the emperor through the analogy "one God—one human ruler." Eusebius later applied this concept to Constantine. Changes within

3. 1 Clement 37; cf. Adolf von Harnack, *Militia Christi* (Darmstadt: Wissenschaftliche Buchgesellschaft, 1963), pp. 18–19.

the church, the growth of congregations, the loss of an eschatological consciousness, the threat from heresy, and oppression
from the Roman state were operative in the church in such a way
that institutionalized authority structures became stronger and
stronger at the expense of the free, prophetic charism. One may
regret this development, but the course of history, especially the
acute conflict in which the church found itself, really made it
unavoidable.

And yet counterforces continued to operate. Thus, when the
author of the Gospel of Matthew, for example, in sharp antithesis
to the growing prestige of the Jewish rabbinate, attacks the
scribes who like "to be greeted respectfully in the street, and to
be addressed as 'rabbi'" (Matt. 23:7, NEB), he also has Christian
dignitaries in mind. The way the passage continues makes that
clear: "But you must not be called 'rabbi'; for you have one
Rabbi, and you are all brothers. Do not call any man on earth
'father'; for you have one Father, and he is in heaven. Nor must
you be called 'teacher'; you have one Teacher, the Messiah" (23:8–
10, NEB). Appended to this material is an authentic saying of
Jesus: "The greatest among you must be your servant" (Matt.
23:11, NEB; cf. Mark 9:35, 10:43–44; Luke 9:48, 22:26).

Here the antipharisaic polemic turns into a clear warning to
leaders in the Christian community. The Gospel of John also
acknowledges no hierarchy or authority structures in the community. It consciously omits the account of the institution of the
Lord's Supper and substitutes the story of the foot-washing.
Could it be, perhaps, that this represents a certain critique against
catholic eucharistic practice as we encounter it in that period in
the letters of Ignatius? The admonition that the Johannine Jesus
gives immediately after the foot-washing speaks for itself: "I have
set you an example: you are to do as I have done for you. In
very truth I tell you, a servant is not greater than his master, nor
a messenger than the one who sent him. If you know this, happy
are you if you act upon it" (13:15–16, NEB).

Since that time the tension between charism and authority
structure within the church has never ceased. Because the mes-

sage of the gospel itself contains both the binding authority of apostolic tradition and the freedom of the Spirit, this tension has been in some measure present in the church from the beginning. After the repression of free charismatic prophecy, which once again had burst forth vigorously during the second half of the second century in the Montanist movement, it was, above all, martyrs and confessors who exercised charismatic authority, even over against the bishops. Later on, in the Constantinian era, ascetics and monks partly took their place. In the Eastern Church some of this noninstitutionalized spiritual power has been preserved among the holy men known as *startsy*. The church had to preserve this tension, which was operative from the beginning, if it wished to maintain its power as "salt of the earth" and "light of the world" (Matt. 5:13 ff.), even if this led frequently to bitter controversies and painful schisms. This tension was a sign that the church's "authority structures" were always subject to the corrective of the gospel, the unmanipulable apostolic *verbum externum* (external word). But this external word is not the letter, which kills, but the Spirit, which gives life (2 Cor. 3:6): "And where the Spirit of the Lord is, there is freedom" (2 Cor. 3:17).

6

The Power of the State and the Authority of the Community

In the first three decades of the church's existence there hardly seem to have been serious conflicts between it and the power of Rome. As the example of Paul shows, the Christian mission was able to develop relatively free of Roman opposition. It was the Neronian persecution of 64 A. D. that first brought a change in this picture, but apparently even that persecution was restricted to Rome. The persecutions that the community experienced between 30 A. D. and the execution of James, the Lord's brother, in 62 A. D. emanated primarily from the Sadducean priestly aristocracy and from King Agrippa I (41–44 A. D.). The pharisees participated only to a limited degree, in the death of Stephen and the expulsion of his companions from Jerusalem (Acts 6:1–8:3) and in the legal action against Paul, for example. They turned above all against those Jewish Christians who had broken with the law. According to his own testimony even Paul had participated, prior to his conversion, in that sort of persecution (Gal. 1:13; Phil. 3:6; 1 Cor. 15:9).

Only after 70 A. D. did the conflict with the newly restored pharisaism intensify, leading to an open break through the anathema against Jewish Christians inserted into the official daily prayer known as the Eighteen Benedictions. Thereby Christians were categorically excluded from synagogue worship. In the Diaspora, the early Christians' intensive missionary activity led at times to clashes with Jewish congregations, which attempted to prevail upon the local authorities to take action against the Christian disturbers of the peace. The expulsion of the Jews (Jewish Christians) from Rome by Claudius in about 48 A. D., reported

by Suetonius,[1] was perhaps occasioned by disturbances of that
kind. To be sure, the Jewish pseudo-Messiah Bar Kokhba (132–
135 A. D.) is said to have persecuted the Christians in Palestine.[2]
And Tertullian, in a frequently quoted lapidary phrase, calls the
Jewish congregations "fountains of persecution" (*synagogas
Judaeorum fontes persecutionum*),[3] but the Christian rigorist may
well have overstated the case. Later on, once the Christians came
to power, fanatics in their midst retaliated against the oppression
of the early period with unlimited severity.

Except in Jewish Palestine the spread of Christianity was certainly not impeded by the Jewish opposition it experienced at the
outset. On the contrary, the mission to the Gentiles was actually
furthered by strained relationships with the Jewish religion from
which Christianity had sprung.

Thus, in view of the situation in the earliest period, it is totally
comprehensible that Paul, in his first letter known to us (1 Thess.
2:14–15), mentions the persecutions of congregations in Thessalonica and Judea by Jews, and, on the other hand, in the famous
passage Romans 13:1–7, urges *obedience to governing authorities,*
since they are "instituted" by God. Here one—the Roman citizen—has recourse to concepts familiar to Greek-speaking Jews in
the Diaspora, who were consciously loyal to the Roman government, since both Julius Caesar and Augustus improved and guaranteed the legal status of Jews in the Roman empire, in contrast
to the arbitrary treatment Jews often received in the Greek city-
states. The only places in the empire in which the lot of the Jews
grew worse were Palestine, Egypt, Cyrenaica, and Cyprus.
Therefore bloody rebellions broke out in these places in 66 and
116 A. D.

The apostle's relatively positive stance toward the power of the
state is further influenced by the fact that the *Pax Romana* established the system of guaranteed (though limited) rights that

1. Suetonius, *Claudius* 25.3; cf. Acts 18:2.
2. Justin, 1 *Apology* 31.6.
3. Tertullian, *Scorpiace* 10.

first made possible the worldwide mission he was carrying on in the fifties. Thus Seneca's brother, Junius Annaeus Gallio, the governor of Achaia, dismissed the charges that members of the local synagogue brought against Paul in Corinth in 51(?) A. D. And, according to Acts 21:31 ff., he was later rescued from a lynch mob in Jerusalem by the Roman commander of the fortress Antonia.

The Pauline injunction to obey the governmental authorities has suffered many a disastrous misinterpretation during the church's history right up to the present, above all in German Lutheranism. Yet one dare not tear the apostle's injunction from its context, understanding it as a confession of the intrinsic metaphysical value of the state. The text is part of the concluding parenetic section of Romans (chaps. 12–14) and is framed by a renunciation of force and the love command. It is most important to note the immediately preceding sentence, to which the injunction of obedience is attached: "Do not be overcome by evil, but overcome evil with good" (Rom. 12:21). Applied to the governmental authorities this means, for the Christians in Rome, loyalty, in fact obedience out of conviction (13:5: "for conscience's sake"), and readiness to pay taxes and to honor those to whom honor is due.

There are, to be sure, two points that one dare not overlook. First of all, as Paul lays the foundation for his ethical parenesis by imploring Christians to offer themselves as a sacrifice to God, he also requires a new kind of "spiritual worship," which occurs through "a renewing of the mind" and trains a person to discern with care (*dokimazein*; cf. Eph. 5:10; Gal. 6:4; Phil. 1:10; 1 Thess. 5:21) what God's will actually is. This also applies to obedience given the state. *What is demanded is no blind, irrational servitude, but a conscious (and thus vigilant and critical) obedience.* Secondly, the call for obedience is followed a few verses later (Rom. 13:11 ff.) by a reference to the *kairos* of the parousia, coming nearer all the time. Thereby—as with the adversative *but* in Jesus' answer to the question about paying taxes to Caesar—the

significance of governmental authorities is limited and relativized.
They are instituted by God and surely necessary and salutary, but
their days are numbered, their significance only transitory.

In addition, the New Testament *clearly limits the command to
be obedient.* In fact, this limitation is made by an author who
also gives a basically positive picture of the Roman government,
presumably during the reign of Domitian (81–96 A. D.), who
again took action against the Christians. In Acts 5:29 Luke has
the apostles say something quite similar to a statement already
made by Socrates in his famous defense:[4] "We must obey God
rather than men." How deeply this conviction influenced Christians is shown about twenty years later by the first report of proceedings against Christians in a letter to the emperor Trajan
written about 111 A. D. by Pliny, the governor of the provinces of
Bithynia and Pontus in Asia Minor: "Meantime this is the course
I have taken with those who were accused before me as Christians. I asked them whether they were Christians, and if they
confessed, I asked them a second and third time with threats of
punishment. If they kept to it, I ordered them for execution; for
I held no question that whatever it was that they admitted, in any
case obstinacy and unbending perversity deserve to be pun-
ished."[5] Pliny's procedure, approved by the emperor, was destined to become typical of the period that followed.

*Despite the constant threat of persecution and the absence of
guaranteed rights* (actual persecutions were, it is true, relatively
infrequent and sporadic in the early period), *Christians remained
loyal to emperor and empire.* First Peter, which also was written
during the reign of Domitian, requires no less clearly than
Romans 13 obedience to the emperor and the governors under
him (2:13–14). At the same time it offers an indirect testimony
to the slanders that were brought against Christians, slanders that
also play a role in Pliny's letter: "For it is God's will that by doing

4. Plato, *Apology* 29d; cf. 37e–38a and Acts 4:19.
5. Pliny, *Epistles* 10.96, quoted from J. Stevenson, ed., *A New Eusebius* (London: SPCK, 1963), p. 13.

right you should put to silence the ignorance of foolish men" (1 Peter 2:15).

The Pastoral Epistles, likely following the custom of Diaspora Judaism, encourage prayer "for all people, for kings and all in authority" (1 Tim. 2:1–2). The pragmatic reason that the author gives indicates, of course, an understandable lessening of the intense eschatological anticipation of the earliest period: "that we may lead a quiet and peaceable life, godly and respectful in every way" (2:2). This emphasis on loyalty to the government, combined with *intercessions for the rulers*, runs like a red thread through the various Christian apologies of the second and third centuries. A typical example is the conclusion of Athenagoras's *Supplication*, addressed to Marcus Aurelius and his son Commodus:

> For who are more deserving to obtain the things they ask, than those who, *like us, pray for your government,* that you may, as is most equitable, receive the kingdom, son from father, and that your empire may receive increase and addition, all men becoming subject to your sway? And this is also for our advantage, that we may lead a peaceable and quiet life [=1 Tim. 2:2; see above!], and may ourselves readily perform all that is commanded us.[6]

It is obvious that intercession for the emperor could also be interpreted quite differently, as Tertullian shows, since he bases it on, among other things, the command to love one's enemies: "Learn from [our Scriptures] that the precept is given us . . . to pray to God even for our enemies, to beseech His blessings for our persecutors. Who are more the enemies and the persecutors of Christians, than those against whose majesty we are accused of treason?"[7]

Thus reference to intercession for the emperor also appears

---

6. Athenagoras, *A Plea for the Christians* 37, in *The Ante-Nicene Fathers,* vol. 2, ed. Alexander Roberts and James Donaldson, rev. A. Cleveland Coxe (Grand Rapids, Mich.: Eerdmans, 1962), p. 148.

7. Tertullian, *Apology* 31.2, trans. T. R. Glover, Loeb Classical Library (Cambridge, Mass.: Harvard University Press, 1960), pp. 153–55; cf. *The Epistle of Polycarp* 12.3.

frequently in the trial reports in the acts of martyrs. The martyr Acacius can ask the governor, "By whom is the emperor loved more than by us?," pointing as evidence to a constant intercession that includes not only peace for the empire but also the welfare of the soldiers.[8]

The Christian Donata, one of the martyrs in Scillium in North Africa (180 A. D.), answers the proconsul Saturninus, "*Honorem Caesari quasi Caesari; timorem autem Deo*"[9] ("Give the emperor the honor that is his as emperor, but fear God [alone];" cf. 1 Peter 2:17). Thus *loyalty to the state had a precise boundary, set down by faith*: Christians had to avoid sacrificing to the emperor, swearing by the genius of the emperor, and cursing Christ, if they did not want to become apostates. When asked by the governor of Asia in 155 A. D. to do precisely that, Polycarp, the aged bishop of Smyrna, answered: "For eighty and six years have I been his servant, and he has done me no wrong, and how can I blaspheme my King who saved me?"[10]

Attachment to the *basileus* Christ is stronger than loyalty to the *basileus* of the empire. That the power of the former king and not that of the emperor determines the course of time and eternity is shown by the authors of *The Martyrdom of Polycarp* who, in dating the martyrdom, put in place of the customary year of the emperor's reign, "while Jesus Christ is reigning (*basileuontos*) forever."[11]

Persecutions kept on erupting for a variety of reasons, two of which merit special attention. First, Christians brought down upon themselves the hatred of the masses by shunning the public religious ceremonies and festivals. People considered them "godless" and levelled the most absurd charges against them, including

8. *Akten des Acacius,* in Knopf-Krüger, *Ausgewählte Märtyrerakten* (Tübingen: J. C. B. Mohr, 1965⁴), p. 57; cf. J. M. Hornus, *Politische Entscheidung in der Alten Kirche. Beiträge zur evangelischen Theologie* 35 (Munich: Kaiser Verlag, 1963), pp. 82–83.

9. Text in Knopf-Krüger, p. 29.

10. *The Martyrdom of Polycarp* 9.3, in *The Apostolic Fathers,* vol. 2, trans. Kirsopp Lake, Loeb Classical Library (Cambridge, Mass.: Harvard University Press, 1959), p. 325.

11. *The Martyrdom of Polycarp* 21.

incest, ritual murder, and cannibalism. These accusations were believed even among the educated. Thus in the dialogue *Octavius* by Minucius Felix, the pagan Caecilius refers to an anti-Christian discourse by the famous rhetorician Fronto[12] which accuses Christians of the wildest orgies. Their "one and only God, solitary, forlorn," is even more wretched than the weak and powerless God of the Jews, since he ended up in the captivity of the Romans. He appears to be a "troublesome, restless, shameless and interfering being, who has a hand in everything that is done," and yet is unable to be of help to anyone.[13] But the principal reproach concerns their shunning of all sorts of activities:

> Have not the Romans without your God empire and rule, do they not enjoy the whole world, and lord it over you? Meanwhile in anxious doubt you deny yourselves wholesome pleasures; you do not attend the shows; you take no part in the processions; fight shy of public banquets; abhor the sacred games, meats from the victims, drinks poured in libation on the altars. So frightened are you of the gods whom you deny![14]

The other basis for the persecutions was *reasons of state*, which saw in the increasing spread of Christianity a danger to internal order. While Trajan and Hadrian could still be (relatively) broad-minded, the philosopher Marcus Aurelius, with an eye toward the more intense threat to the empire from outside and the catastrophes, plague, and famine within, believed that he was obliged to intensify the proceedings against the Christians, since they threatened the stability of the empire. Finally Septimius Severus is said to have issued an edict prohibiting conversion to Christianity (202 A. D.), and Decius and Diocletian each combined the attempt to restore the empire with a very intensive persecution of Christians (250 and 303 A. D.). The final, most intense persecution lasted for eight years before it ended through the edict of toleration of Galerius in 311 A. D.

12. Minucius Felix, *Octavius* 9.6, 31.2, trans. Gerald H. Rendall, Loeb Classical Library (Cambridge, Mass.: Harvard University Press, 1960).
13. Minucius Felix, *Octavius* 10.3–5, p. 341.
14. Ibid. 12.5, pp. 345–47.

The early church's relationship to the power of the Roman state could also be viewed, of course, under the *negative* aspect of *irreconcilable opposition.* When the governor urged him to swear by the genius of the emperor (*per genium domini nostri imperatoris*), Speratus, the spokesman for the martyrs of Scillium, answered: "I do not recognize the empire [*imperium*] of this world; but rather I serve that God, whom no man has seen nor can see. I have not stolen, but if I buy anything, I pay the tax, because I recognize my Lord, the King of kings and Emperor [*imperator*] of all peoples" (cf. Rev. 19:16, 1:5: *"princeps regum terrae"* [ruler of the kings of the earth]).[15] Later Cittinus added: "We have none other to fear save the Lord our God who is in heaven."[16]

Thereby the emperor, as *imperator* and *dominus* of the earthly *imperium,* is set in clear opposition to the Christians' heavenly Lord, to whom the designation *imperator* is here applied for the first time. Even paying taxes is done only in obedience to his command and not out of loyalty to the earthly emperor. In the martyr acts of Bishop Fructuosus, from the time of the Valerian persecution (259 A. D.), the bishop responds to the governor's question of whether he knows the commands of the emperor: "I do not know his commands: I am a Christian!" As Fructuosus confesses his faith in the one God, the Creator and Lord of the world, and denies the existence of the gods, the governor cries out in disgust: "Who will be obeyed [at all any more], who will be feared and venerated [at all any more]? If people don't esteem the gods, neither will the images of the emperor be venerated."[17]

The trial in the martyr acts of the soldier Dasius, at the time of Diocletian, focuses the issues even more pointedly. When asked his name, the soldier responds, "My real name is Christian; the name my parents gave me is Dasius."

Then the legate Bassus urges, "Venerate the images of our

15. *The Martyrs of Scillium,* in J. Stevenson, ed., *A New Eusebius* (London: SPCK, 1963), p. 42.
16. Ibid.
17. Text in Knopf-Krüger, p. 83 (lines 20 ff.).

lords, the emperors, who give us peace, who furnish our pay and see to our welfare each day!"

Dasius refuses: "I am not a soldier of an earthly king but of a heavenly King. I have received his wages, I live by his grace and am rich through his inexpressible love for humanity."

Refusing to give up, the governor tries once more: "Don't you know, Dasius, that everyone is subject to the imperial command and the sacred laws?"

The soldier answers, "Go ahead and do what is commanded you by the godless and foul emperors . . ." The entire trial ends with this sharp reply: "Do what you want, I am a Christian. I spit on and abominate your emperors and their glory, so that after release from this life I can attain the life to come."[18]

Thus it is quite understandable that the earliest literary polemic against Christians of which we have any record, written by the Platonist Celsus, contains the reproach that the Christian refusal to serve "several masters . . . is a rebellious utterance [*staseōs phōnä*] of people who . . . wall themselves off and break away from the rest of mankind."[19] This inclination to rebel is in Celsus's view basically something Christians inherited from the Jews, for the Jews rebelled against the Egyptians at the exodus. Now the Christians have repaid them in kind,[20] which is not surprising since the founder of the Christian sect was a revolutionary. He and his followers belong to the dregs of society. "Celsus was, as far as we can tell, the first to attribute to Christianity, in a negative sense to be sure, a pronounced 'theology of revolution.'"[21]

That these and similar reproaches surely had a long prehistory is proven by the fact that Luke, in Jesus' trial before Pilate, has the Jewish leaders say that "he stirs up the people" and "forbids

18. Text in Knopf-Krüger, *Ausgewählte Märtyrerakten*, pp. 93–94; cf. Hornus, *Politische Entscheidung*, pp. 126–27.

19. Origen, *Contra Celsum* 8.2, trans. Henry Chadwick (Cambridge: Cambridge University Press, 1965), p. 454 (cf. 8.49).

20. Ibid. 3.5–10.

21. Karlmann Beyschlag, "Christentum und Veränderung in der Alten Kirche," *Kerygma und Dogma* 18 (1972):38; cf. Origen, *Contra Celsum* 3.55, 59; 4:23 ff.; 5.63. See also Erik Peterson, "Der Monotheismus als politisches Problem," in *Theologische Traktate* (Munich: Kösel, 1951), pp. 79 ff.

us to pay taxes to Caesar" (Luke 23:5, 2). According to Acts
17:7, the Jews in Thessalonica are said to have made the accusation against Paul and Silas, "They all flout the Emperor's laws and
assert that there is a rival king, Jesus" (NEB). That Luke, so
loyal to the Roman state, included this slander in his work shows
that it was said at his time by those hostile to Christianity. The
reign of Christ and of the emperor could thus also be understood
to be in opposition.

A sharply accented, critical, and implacable stance toward
Roman rule and the emperor appears for the first time in the Book
of Revelation, written during Domitian's reign, as were 1 Peter
(so different in stance) and the two volumes by Luke. There is
in Revelation, on the one hand, a continuation of the harsh anti-
Roman tradition of Jewish apocalyptic, which we also find in
Syriac Baruch and 4 Ezra, apocalypses from the same period. On
the other hand, however, Revelation is no longer Jewish and theocratic in orientation; rather it is thoroughly *Christocentric*. Further, we meet therein, step by step, "the supplanting of the
emperor by Christ."[22] This begins with the opening vision
(1:9 ff.), continues with the great visions of heaven in chapters
4 and 5, and reaches its climax in the depiction of the beast from
the abyss and its false prophet, the two anti-Christ figures, in
chapter 13, and of "Babylon the whore," the metropolis of Rome,
in chapter 17. The destruction of the godless power and its
accomplices happens miraculously in a "final battle." The returning Christ appears here, in total conformity with Jewish models,
as the warrior Messiah on a white horse; "from his mouth there
went a sharp sword with which to smite the nations" (Rev. 19:15,
NEB; cf. Isa. 11:4). The depiction of the bloody annihilation of
all God's enemies shows the animosity, indeed the hatred, the seer
has for the power of Rome:

> Then I saw the beast and the kings of the earth and their armies
> mustered to do battle with the Rider and his army. The beast
> was taken prisoner, and so was the false prophet. . . .   The two of

22. A. A. T. Ehrhardt, *Politische Metaphysik von Solon bis Augustin,* vol.
2, *Die christliche Revolution* (Tübingen: J. C. B. Mohr, 1959), p. 26.

them were thrown alive into the lake of fire with its sulphurous flames. The rest were killed by the sword which went out of the Rider's mouth; and all the birds gorged themselves on their flesh. [19:19–21, NEB]

The millennium that follows brings the earthly reign of Christ in a peaceful world in which Satan is bound. Chiliasm, which also grows out of Jewish eschatology, gets its New Testament support in this section of the book of Revelation. In the second century chiliasm was extremely popular in the church, especially in Asia Minor. It began to be repressed in the third century through the theology of Origen, but again and again in the church's history it found new adherents among outsiders, since it offered the possibility of combining sociopolitical aspirations with the Christian expectation for the future. Karl Barth's statement, "Without chiliasm—even if it were only a pinch—no ethics,"[23] is worth considering in this context, even though in Article 17 of the Augsburg Confession the historical myth of a millennial reign of the Messiah on earth was properly rejected as "Jewish opinions" (*iudaicae opiniones*). And yet even in the Book of Revelation the oppressed community was not to take matters into its own hands by resorting to violence. Judgment on the enemies of God is reserved solely for the returning Christ. He needs no human help to establish his kingdom. The task of the persecuted community is not to do battle with the sword but to bear faithful witness and to persevere in suffering: "Whoever is to be made prisoner, a prisoner shall he be. Whoever takes the sword to kill, by the sword he is bound to be killed. This is where the fortitude and faithfulness of God's people have their place" (Rev. 13:10, NEB).

The intransigent attitude toward the ruling world power and its leader is concentrated in the tradition about the *antichrist*. He is already hinted at in the little apocalypse in Mark (13:14) and attains clear features in the deutero-Pauline second letter to the Thessalonians. There he brings the final rebellion against God and is revealed as wickedness in human form, "the man

23. "Das Problem der Ethik in der Gegenwart," in *Das Wort Gottes und ⁚ Theologie* (Munich: Kaiser Verlag, 1924), p. 140.

doomed to perdition. He is the Enemy. He rises in his pride against every god, so called, every object of men's worship, and even takes his seat in the temple of God claiming to be a god himself" (2 Thess. 2:3–4, NEB).

As in the Jewish prophetic tradition, this end-time figure is regarded as the final representative of the evil world power. The Jewish Sibylline oracles from that period identify this figure with, among others, Nero, who was expected to come back to life. The *Didache* calls him "the deceiver of the world" who, claiming to be a "Son of God," shall do signs and wonders, "and the earth shall be delivered into his hands."[24] Here, as in the Apocalypse of John, the forces of evil in the political sphere increase until the consummation, when a ruler assumes the form of a diabolical antitype of Christ and subjugates the entire world. The persecutions that kept breaking out, and the demand, usually put to Christians during their trials, that they worship the emperor, make it understandable that in certain Christian circles the Roman government was understood to be the antichrist, or at the very least his forerunner. And yet responsible theologians such as Irenaeus avoided a short-circuited identification of that kind: "Earthly rule, therefore, has been appointed by God for the benefit of nations—and not by the devil, who is never at rest at all, nay, who does not love to see even nations conducting themselves after a quiet manner—so that under the fear of human rule, men may not eat each other up like fishes."[25]

This realistic understanding comes relatively close to Paul's in Romans 13, a chapter to which Irenaeus attaches great importance. In his interpretation of this chapter he does not, of course, set up the state as part of God's "order of creation," but as a provisional arrangement necessitated by the fall into sin: "For since man, by departing from God, reached such a pitch of fury

---

24. *Didache,* 16.4.

25. Irenaeus, *Against Heresies* 5.24.2, in *The Ante-Nicene Fathers,* vol. 1, ed. Alexander Roberts and James Donaldson, rev. A. Cleveland Coxe (Grand Rapids, Mich.: Eerdmans, 1962), p. 552 (altered slightly).

as even to look upon his brother as his enemy, and engaged without fear . . . in murder and avarice, God imposed upon mankind the fear of man, as they did not acknowledge the fear of God."[26]

The devil is lying, therefore, when he claims that the powers of this world have been given to him and that he is able to give them to whomever he chooses.[27]   God is also the Lord over kings and executes his judgment through them:

> For by the law of the same Being as calls men into existence are kings also appointed, adapted for those men who are at the time placed under their government.   Some of these [rulers] are given for the correction and the benefit of their subjects and for the preservation of justice; but others, for the purposes of fear and punishment and rebuke: others, as [the subjects] deserve it, are for deception, disgrace, and pride; while the just judgment of God . . . passes equally upon all.[28]

Thus Irenaeus is also able to emphasize the positive side of the Roman state: "Through [the] instrumentality [of the Romans] the world is at peace, and we walk on the highways without fear, and sail where we will."[29]

One ought not, of course, misunderstand all this as a truly positive stance toward the Roman empire.   It is true that Irenaeus acknowledges even the possibility of living as a Christian in the palace of the emperor.[30]   But there is no way that one can speak of genuine political cooperation with the empire by Christians. "For in the political power of the Roman empire lay . . . fertile seeds of the future reign of the antichrist, and Satan was constantly lying in wait to take up this reign."[31]   Therefore Irenaeus's discussion of world powers on the basis of Romans 13 is followed immediately by the presentation about the antichrist.[32]   With deepest fervor the Bishop of Lyons awaited the inauguration of

26. Ibid.
27. Ibid. 5.24.1, 3, following Luke 4:6.
28. Ibid. 5.24.3, p. 552.
29. Ibid. 4.30.3, p. 503.
30. Ibid. 4.30.1.
31. Ehrhardt, *Politische Metaphysik*, p. 114.
32. Irenaeus, *Against Heresies* 5.25–30.

the thousand-year reign of Christ. The church needed to prepare
itself for this alone.

Based on his own calculations, Hippolytus, who was active in
Rome a little later, awaited the kingdom of God only in the more
distant future, and therefore hated Rome all the more intensely.
Following the Apocalypse of John he identifies Rome with the
dreadful fourth beast in Daniel 7:7 ff. Thereby political power
became practically identical with the godless "world." Church
and Roman empire, both developing during the reign of Augustus,
stand in sharp, irreconcilable contrast: Christ created his new
people, Christians, from all nations, while Satan gave the Romans
dominion over the world. It is true that even Hippolytus could
not identify the empire directly with the antichrist's kingdom,
since this was supposed to appear only in the future, but the
empire prepared its way and bore its marks.[33]

Lactantius, the confidant of Constantine and tutor of his son
Crispus, still held a similar critical judgment of Rome at the
beginning of the fourth century. The Roman empire appeared
to him in danger of falling to pieces—as it deserved to do. The
antichrist would then build his kingdom on its ruins.[34]

After looking at this at times thoroughgoing animosity toward
the power of Rome one could ask with Wilhelm Weber "*why
[Christianity] did not seek to do battle against the state,* the
thought of the coming destruction of the empire inspiring them
all and a fighting spirit carrying them away to the point of self-
sacrifice."[35] Weber points to the example of the Jews, who in three
bloody rebellions within a span of seventy years sought freedom
from the "godless rule"—to use the wording of the Jewish prayers—
and, beyond that, sought to force the *arrival* of the messianic
kingdom.

That Christians were well aware of this problem is shown by

---

33 Ehrhardt, *Politische Metaphysik,* pp. 125 ff.

34. Ibid., pp. 235–36, 243–44; Hornus, *Politische Entscheidung,* pp. 47 ff.

35. "Nec nostri saeculi est," in Richard Klein, ed., *Das frühe Christentum im römischen Staat, Wege der Forschung* 267 (Darmstadt: Wissenschaftliche Buchgesellschaft, 1971), p. 31 (italics mine).

Tertullian's reflections on the possibility of active and passive Christian opposition to the power of the Roman state:

> For if we wished to play the part of open enemies, and not merely hidden avengers, should we lack the power that numbers and battalions give? . . . We are but of yesterday, and we have filled everything you have—cities, islands, forts, towns, exchanges, yes! and camps, . . . palace, senate, forum. All we have left to you is the temples! . . . For what war should we not have been fit and ready even if unequal in forces—we who are so glad to be butchered—were it not, of course, that in our doctrine we are given ampler liberty to be killed than to kill?
>
> Why! without taking up arms, without rebellion, simply by standing aside, by mere ill-natured separation, we could have fought you! For if so vast a mass of people as we had broken away from you and removed to some recess of the world apart, the mere loss of so many citizens of whatever sort would have brought a blush to your rule. . . . You would have had to look about for people to rule. You would have had more enemies left than citizens.[36]

The renunciation of force expressed here has its roots not only in the injunctions Jesus gives in the Sermon on the Mount but also in a Christian "political" self-understanding that Paul had already expressed with the audacious statement, "Our citizenship is in heaven" (Phil. 3:20), and which the author of Hebrews caught with the words, "For here we have no lasting city [*polis*, or city-state], but we seek the city which is to come" (13:14). Since Christians are not citizens of an earthly realm, they cannot fight with the means of exercising power common to such realms, with weapons and emigration. Tertullian can express this self-understanding in Stoic fashion: "nothing is more foreign to us than the State. One state we know, of which all are citizens—the universe."[37]

At this point we need to refer to an incident in the New Testament. Central for the political theology of early Christianity, this incident demonstrates as no other the early Christian relationship to earthly power: it is *Jesus' conversation with Pilate,* recorded in

36. Tertullian, *Apology* 37.4 ff., pp. 169–71 (Loeb edition).
37. Ibid. 38.3, p. 173.

John 18:33–38. This is certainly not a historical report of what
was actually said. The oldest account of the trial, in Mark
15:2–15, has nothing about a lengthy dialogue between Jesus and
Pilate; instead it reports that Jesus was silent. Besides, John's
account bears clear marks of Johannine theology and terminology:

> Jesus replied, "My kingdom [*basileia*] does not belong to this
> world. If it did, my followers would be fighting to save me from
> arrest by the Jews. My kingly authority comes from elsewhere."
> "You are a king, then?" said Pilate. Jesus answered, " 'King' is
> your word. My task is to bear witness to the truth. For this was
> I born; for this I came into the world, and all who are not deaf to
> truth listen to my voice." Pilate said, "What is truth?" [John
> 18:36–38, NEB]

Behind the Fourth Evangelist's way of presenting Jesus' trial
before Pilate stands a long tradition. The starting point was the
condemnation and crucifixion of Jesus as an alleged "king of the
Jews," which forced the community to face again and again the
charge that Jesus really had been a political revolutionary (cf.
John 19:12). In that context they could recall reports that Jesus,
when urged by the crowd to seize political power, had actually
withstood the temptation. For according to John 6:14–15, he
refused the crowd's attempt to take him by force "to make him
king" after the feeding of the five thousand. According to the
story of Jesus' temptation preserved in Q, the early collection of
Jesus' sayings (Matt. 4:8 ff. = Luke 4:5 ff.), Jesus rejects Satan's
offer to make him ruler of the world.

A strange parallel from that period is offered in Hegesippus's
report, preserved by Eusebius, of the trial of the Palestinian
grandnephews of Jesus before the emperor Domitian. Domitian
had them brought to Rome as descendants of David and asked
them whether they were of Davidic descent and how much
property they had. They responded that they were humble
farmers, and then they "were asked concerning the Christ and his
kingdom, its nature, origin, and time of appearance, and explained
*that it was neither of the world nor earthly, but heavenly and
angelic,* and it would be at the end of the world, when he would

come in glory to judge the living and the dead and to reward every man according to his deeds."[38]

Also for the Fourth Evangelist Jesus' realm is a transcendent power that has nothing to do with earthly kingdoms that defend their existence with brute force. On the other hand, in keeping with this evangelist's particular theology, the picture of the future kingdom gives place to a realized eschatology. Whoever believes Jesus' witness to the truth "has hold of eternal life, and does not come up for judgment, but has already passed from death to life" (John 5:24, NEB; cf. 11:25–26).

Since the concept of Jesus' *basileia* occurs in the Gospel of John only in the trial before Pilate, it may be a traditional picture which the evangelist, in his own fashion, applies to the present salvation that comes by faith. The testimony of Jesus the king (*basileus*) to God's truth finds its culmination, paradoxically, in his way of suffering, leading to the cross. John can describe the crucifixion as "exaltation" and "glorification" (3:14; 8:28; 12:32, 34; 12:23, 28; 17:1, and elsewhere). In obedience Jesus takes this way upon himself, and thus he himself is "the truth and the life" (14:6). Pilate's famous question concluding the conversation is not to be understood psychologically or philosophically. It is meant to demonstrate total misunderstanding on the part of a person who counts on and lives by the power of "this world" alone.

Oswald Spengler, who was particularly fascinated by Jesus' conversation with Pilate, stresses the sharp contrast between the two figures: "When Jesus was taken before Pilate, then *the world of facts and the world of truths were face to face in immediate and implacable hostility*. It is a scene appallingly distinct and overwhelming in its symbolism, such as the world's history had never before and has never since looked at."[39] Over against Spengler's statement it must be stressed that the text does not speak of "truths" in the sense of timeless ideas but of the one

38. Eusebius, *The Ecclesiastical History*, vol. 1, 3.20, trans. Kirsopp Lake, Loeb Classical Library (Cambridge, Mass.: Harvard University Press, 1959), p. 239 (italics mine).

39. Oswald Spengler, *The Decline of the West*, vol. 2, trans. C. F. Atkinson (New York: Alfred A. Knopf, 1947), p. 216 (italics mine).

truth of God, which alone can give human life its meaning and basis. On the other hand, the use of political power for its own sake is in the final analysis futile, as Pilate's own fate shows. When Spengler finally characterizes Pilate's question as "the one word that is race-pure in the whole New Testament,"[40] this only shows that, blinded by the spirit of his time, he has misunderstood it completely.

And yet in interpreting this scene one cannot stop with the contrast between earthly, human power and God's truth, which is not of this world, not at man's disposal. For one thing, the Fourth Evangelist, like Paul in Romans 13, knows that the earthly powers' ability to rule is dependent on the will of God. When Pilate asks, "Surely you know that I have authority to release you, and I have authority to crucify you?" Jesus responds, "You would have no authority at all over me . . . if it had not been granted you from above" (John 19:10–11, NEB). Secondly, the mission, message, and way of Jesus show that God loves this world (3:16), despite its failure to live in dependence upon him, and that as the witness to the truth Jesus, bearing his own cross (19:17), "takes away the sin of the world" (1:29). His parting cry in the Fourth Gospel, "It is finished" (19:30), is a cry of victory. "The prince of this world *is* judged" (16:11). In the light of this event the evangelist's disciples confess, *"This is the victory that overcomes the world, our faith"* (1 John 5:4).

40. Ibid.

7

Toward the Establishment of the Imperial Church

The world, of course, was destined to appear as the stronger. Neither opposition to the earthly powers nor even their conquest determined the church's future course. Rather, more and more, its course was determined by the thought of moving toward an *alliance with the world power*. In spite of the intensification of massive persecutions in the third century, the Roman empire did not come to be identified as the antichrist. Instead, in the fourth century the church became "the imperial church," not in an earthly-millennial *regnum Christi* but in a thoroughly human *regnum mundi*. The way Christianity went led not to "the reign of Christ" but to participation in the very worldly reign of the Roman empire.

We already encounter the beginnings of this convergence near the end of the first century in the positive presentation of Roman officers and officials in Luke-Acts, and then especially in 1 Clement. In that letter, in a prayer probably taken over from Diaspora Judaism, there is first a petition for universal peace: "Give concord and peace to us and to all that dwell on the earth, as thou didst give to our fathers . . ." This is quite logically followed by intercession for the rulers:

> Grant that we may be obedient to thy almighty and glorious name, and to our rulers and governors upon the earth. Thou, Master, hast given the power of sovereignty to them through thy excellent and inexpressible might, that we may know the glory and honour given to them by thee, and be subject to them, in nothing resisting thy will. And to them, Lord, grant health, peace, concord, firmness that they may administer the government which thou hast given them without offence. For thou, heavenly

51

Master, king of eternity, hast given to the sons of men glory and honour and power over the things which are on the earth; do thou, O Lord, direct their counsels according to that which is "good and pleasing" before thee, that they may administer *with piety [eusebōs]* in peace and gentleness the power given them by thee, and may find mercy in thine eyes.[1]

Not only are divine and human rule bound most closely together here, but prayer is also offered that the rulers might be truly pious. One could ask if the congregation that prayed in this way hoped for the emperor's conversion rather than just his tolerance. Over a hundred years later Tertullian, on the contrary, held the opposite opinion; the emperor, though necessary for the world, could not possibly be a Christian;[2] otherwise Tiberius would have come to faith as Pilate related to him the events that took place in Palestine. Thus Clement's positive attitude toward the Roman empire and its rulers must appear all the more striking. Christian Eggenberger saw in it "a restrained acknowledgement of *Roma aeterna*."[3]

A new development appears in the second half of the second century. Fully conscious of opposition to the pagan state, the apologists sought by their petitions to various emperors tolerance from the state and legal guarantees for the Christians. These writers stressed, in addition to loyalty and legitimacy, the ethical advantages and usefulness of Christians for the empire.

Melito of Sardis, who in about 170 A. D. directed an apology to the philosopher-emperor Marcus Aurelius, who had made harsher regulations against the Christians, brings to bear a new argument—one could say a "salvation-history argument":

> Our philosophy first grew up among the [Jewish] barbarians [that is, non-Greeks], but its full flower came among your nation in the

1. 1 Clement 60.4–61.2, in *The Apostolic Fathers*, vol. 1, trans. Kirsopp Lake, Loeb Classical Library (Cambridge, Mass.: Harvard University Press, 1942), pp. 115–17 (italics mine).

2. Tertullian, *Apology* 21.24; see J. M. Hornus, *Politische Entscheidung in der Alten Kirche. Beiträge zur evangelischen Theologie* 35 (Munich: Kaiser Verlag, 1963), p. 53.

3. Christian Eggenberger, *Die Quellen der politischen Ethik des 1. Clemensbriefes* (Zürich: Zwingli-Verlag, 1951), p. 23.

great reign of your ancestor Augustus, and became an omen of good to your empire, for from that time the power of the Romans became great and splendid. You are now his happy successor, and shall be so along with your son, if you protect the philosophy which grew up with the empire and began with Augustus. Your ancestors nourished it together with the other cults . . .[4]

Even prior to this, Justin had asserted that Christians, in keeping with Jesus' love command, did not hate their persecutors but much rather desired to bring them to conversion and eternal salvation.[5] Moreover, he believed that the world, and thus also the Roman empire, was kept from destruction by fire only for the sake of the Christians.[6] Melito goes one step further: church and empire stand in a historically demonstrable positive relationship to one another.

It is probably also no accident that the first reports of *Christians serving in the army* emerge toward the end of the second century, if one excludes the account of the centurion Cornelius in Acts 10. Luke is also on this point the forerunner of a later development. Celsus, with a measure of justification, reproaches his Christian opponent because of his persistent refusal to serve in the army: "If everyone were to do the same as you, there would be nothing to prevent him [the emperor] from being abandoned, alone and deserted, while earthly things would come into the power of the most lawless and savage barbarians, and nothing more would be heard among men either of your worship [that is, the Christian religion] or of the true wisdom [that is, Platonic philosophy]."[7] And yet in the same period in which these words were written we find Christian legionnaires in the Thundering Legion during Marcus Aurelius's campaign against the Quadi in 173 B. C. The unit came from Melitene on the Syrian-Armenian

A.D.

---

4. Eusebius, *The Ecclesiastical History* 4.26.4–11, vol. 1, trans. Kirsopp Lake, Loeb Classical Library (Cambridge, Mass.: Harvard University Press, 1959), pp. 389, 391.

5. Justin, *1 Apology* 57.1.

6. Justin, *2 Apology* 7.1.

7. Origen, *Contra Celsum* 8.68, trans. Henry Chadwick (Cambridge: Cambridge University Press, 1965), p. 504.

border. In the same region the client-prince Abgar IX, the king
of Edessa (179–216 A. D.), became a Christian and made Christianity the state religion in his territory. Even as a Christian, of
course, he could not renounce the use of arms.

Nevertheless the question of whether and in what form military
service was possible for Christians was fiercely contested into the
fourth century. In the West and in the threatened border
provinces one was more inclined to make compromises than in the
peaceful Greek-speaking provinces. Moreover, it is necessary to
distinguish the ideal of faith from the practice of the communities.
In any case, according to the church order of Hippolytus of Rome,
a baptized soldier had to commit himself neither to carry out exe-
cutions nor to take military oaths. A catechumen or a Christian
who voluntarily reported for military service was excommuni-
cated.[8] Even Origen answers the reproach of Celsus mentioned
above, and his exhortation to Christians "to help the emperor with
all our power, and cooperate with him in what is right, and fight
for him, and be fellow-soldiers if he presses for this," with the
argument that *through their prayers* the Christians are rendering
the emperor "divine help" that is more effective than fighting with
arms. Origen writes, *"We do not become fellow-soldiers with
him, even if he presses for this,* yet we are fighting for him and
composing a special army of piety through our intercessions to
God."[9]

With like consistency Origen interprets the wars in the Old
Testament in a spiritual sense. They cannot be used as a justification for the military profession, since Christ "has come to bring
peace."[10] *And yet there was a shift here in the attitude of Christians.* They prayed not only for the emperor and the preservation
of peace but also for the army and its victory. Even Tertullian

8. A. A. T. Ehrhardt, *Politische Metaphysik von Solon bis Augustin*, vol.
2, *Die christliche Revolution* (Tübingen: J. C. B. Mohr, 1959), p. 125;
Roland Bainton, "The Early Church and War," *Harvard Theological Review*
39 (1946): 191 ff.

9. Origen, *Contra Celsum* 8.73, p. 509 (Chadwick translation; italics
mine).

10. Origen, *De Principiis* 4.14; Hornus, *Politische Entscheidung*, pp. 58–59.

emphasized: "We are ever making intercession for all the Emperors. We pray for them a long life, a secure rule . . . *brave armies* . . ."[11]

From the time of Paul Christendom was also aware that the state "does not bear the sword in vain" (Rom. 13:4). In this world dominated by sin, peace and order can be maintained in the empire only if the state uses force. Even Origen knew this. Since the Christians pray for the victory of the emperor over his enemies, they justify this fighting: "[We pray] for soldiers who fight *justly* and for the ruler who reigns *justly*."[12] And Origen goes even further. He demands for Christians, as the true priests of God, the same privilege accorded the pagan priests, who do not take part in battle:

> It is also your opinion that the priests of certain images and wardens of the temples of the gods . . . should keep their right hand undefiled for the sake of the sacrifices. . . . And in fact when war comes you do not enlist the priests. If, then, this is reasonable, how much more reasonable is it that, while others fight, Christians should also be fighting as priests and worshippers of God, keeping their hands pure and [striving] by their prayers to God . . .[13]

Herman Dörries makes the appropriate comment, "This was more than a contribution to the *pax romana*, it was a spiritual support of the war . . ., a secret and mighty auxiliary for the emperor in a just war."[14]

Thus, in spite of his rejection of military service, this same Origen was able to continue Melito's political-salvation history thinking about a positive relationship between church and empire; indeed he connected this thinking with *an interpretation of the Pax Romana as a preparation for the gospel*:

11. Tertullian, *Apology* 30.4, trans. T. R. Glover, Loeb Classical Library (Cambridge, Mass.: Harvard University Press, 1960), p. 151 (italics mine).

12. *Contra Celsum* 8.73.

13. *Contra Celsum* 8.73 (Chadwick translation).

14. Herman Dörries, *Constantine the Great,* trans. Roland H. Bainton (New York: Harper and Row, 1972), p. 110.

For "righteousness arose in [Jesus'] days and abundance of peace" began with his birth; God was preparing the nations for his teaching, that they might be under one Roman emperor, so that the unfriendly attitude of the nations to one another, caused by the existence of a large number of kingdoms, might not make it more difficult for Jesus' apostles to do what he commanded them when he said "Go and teach all nations." . . . It would have hindered Jesus' teaching from being spread through the whole world if there had been many kingdoms . . . also because men everywhere would have been compelled to do military service and to fight in defence of their own land. . . . Accordingly how could this teaching, which preaches peace and does not even allow men to take vengeance on their enemies, have had any success unless the international situation had everywhere been changed and a milder spirit prevailed at the advent of Jesus?[15]

For the first preeminent Christian theologian and philosopher there was no doubt that in the near future all people would turn to Christ and the other religions cease: "All other worship would be done away and only that of the Christians would prevail. One day it will be the only one to prevail, since the word is continually gaining possession of more souls."[16] At the end stands the universal divine kingdom, prepared for by Roman rule and yet founded solely on the power of the word of Christ. It will include the Roman empire as well as the barbarian peoples. Emperor and empire, despite all opposition to this development, must serve for the establishment of Christ's kingdom of peace.

One might think these words were actually fulfilled two generations later, though to be sure differently from Origen's expectation. The Edict of Toleration of 311 A. D. and the *military victory of Constantine* which followed, first in the West, in 312 A. D. at the Milvian Bridge near Rome, and then twelve years later near Adrianople and Chrysopolis in the East, brought not only an end to terror and insecurity over rights but, positively, *assistance for the church that went beyond mere toleration.*

We need not discuss here the reasons for this transformation.

---

15. *Contra Celsum* 2.30, p. 92 (Chadwick translation); cf. 4.22.
16. Ibid. 8.68, p. 505 (Chadwick translation).

Still less is it our business to render a moral judgment on this eminent and yet shadowy ruler. There are many reasons, some of them going back to his childhood, for Constantine's deliberate turn from the syncretistic monotheism of the sun-god, *Sol invictus,* to the Christian faith. There can be no doubt that he was impressed very early by the Christians' perseverance, their high ethical standards and, above all, by their disciplined community structure, which remained stable even under persecution. For a long time the church had incorporated into its structure the organizational strength of Roman legal thinking. The writings of Cyprian show, for example, that the procedure followed at ecclesiastical assemblies was based heavily on the parliamentary procedure of the Roman senate.[17] The church more and more approximated a state within a state organizationally—a state, to be sure, whose authority depended not on outward force but on the power of faith.

In the final analysis it was the religious power of this Christian faith and not simply political calculation that convinced Constantine of the truth of Christianity. The failure of the last and most severe persecution, initiated by Diocletian, was already recognized by his successor Galerius shortly before his death. The Edict of Toleration in 311 was his work, scarcely influenced by Constantine. The spiritual power of the faith of the Christians had proven stronger than force used by the state.

Therefore, in the face of the negative judgment on the Constantinian era that is so popular at present, we dare not overlook its fundamentally positive significance, still valid today: Constantine "drew Christians from their passive loyalty into an active share in the political life of the state."[18] It was he who first conferred on the Christians, who formerly had remained aloof within the state, real political responsibility in the empire. "When the head of the state, then, was no longer a persecutor but was

---

17. J. Vogt, "Constantinus der Grosse," *Reallexikon für Antike und Christentum,* vol. 3, ed. Theodor Klauser (Stuttgart: Hiersemann, 1957), col. 311.

18. Dörries, *Constantine the Great,* p. 55.

inviting the Christians to share in the administration, could they decline? The old answers were no longer adequate. On the other hand, the sound Christian core of those answers was not to be repudiated. There was, therefore, no easy answer, and we need not be surprised when the answers actually given made this point plain."[19]   That is, the victory, which astounded even the Christians and radically altered the situation, brought entirely new and unexpected tasks and problems, and at the same time also involved the beginnings of an ominous new destiny.

Through the transformation initiated by the young emperor, as A. A. T. Ehrhardt correctly stresses, "the church's old conflict with the empire was turned into a conflict within the empire between the church and the political power of the state."[20]   This conflict could operate in a twofold way. On the one hand, imperial authorities misused the church for their own political ends and used it to confirm and support what those in power wanted. On the other hand, the church used the state's means of power for its own spiritual mission, thereby transforming it into anything but a spiritual mission, whether through the forced "conversion" of those of other faiths or through the imposition of "the unity of the church" by means of the persecution and expulsion of heretics. The situation became most dangerous when church and state no longer had any awareness of the "conflict" which broke out in such a misuse of power, but, oblivious to the need to maintain some distance, sacrificed hand in hand to the gods of power, since in "this world" success alone justifies, and an alleged good end hallows every means.

In what follows I can develop no further the increasingly disastrous entanglement of spiritual and political power. It was not until the Reformation and the Enlightenment that this snarl began to unravel. I would like to go into only three themes: political monotheism, the political Christ, and the start, in Augustine, of a theological interpretation of the new situation.

There was an old philosophical tradition going back to Aristotle

19. Ibid., p. 111.
20. Ehrhardt, *Politische Metaphysik*, p. 259.

that appealed to a quote, originally political in intent, from Homer's *Iliad*: "Lordship for many is no good thing. Let there be one ruler,"[21] to establish the "monarchy" of the highest god. A later Hellenistic variant makes the sole supremacy of the one god, who rules over the lesser gods, analogous to the one ruler on earth. The concept of the divine "monarchy" thus became the ideological support for the ruler ideology of late antiquity.

Even the Montanist Tertullian, truly no friend of the emperors, had stressed that Christians honor the emperor *ut hominem a Deo secundum*, as a person second only to God. "For thus—as less only than the true God—he is greater than all besides."[22] This definition is a monotheistic variant of a pagan notion we encounter, for instance, in the expression from the *Corpus Hermeticum*, "The emperor is the first among men and the last among the gods."[23] It was easy to use this analogy between the divine and imperial monarchy as the "metaphysical" basis for the new Christian empire. In the learned Origenist Eusebius of Caesarea Constantine found his "theological ideologist." He deepened Origen's thesis that the reign of Augustus and the *Pax Romana* established by him prepared the way for the incarnation of the Logos: the "monarchy" had defeated the demonic "polyarchy," the reign of many. The evil fate of all later emperors, who allowed themselves to be carried away by the demons into persecuting Christians, proved the wisdom and justice of divine Providence. Its goal was the establishment of the divine law on earth and its principal tool Constantine, who by his care for the church and the spread of the gospel presented himself as the "universal bishop" whom God himself had consecrated to his office.[24]

The empire, the *Pax Romana*—which had become a *Pax Christiana*—and the divine and earthly monarchy became united har-

21. *The Iliad of Homer* 2.204, trans. Richmond Lattimore (Chicago: University of Chicago Press, 1962), p. 81.
22. Tertullian, *To Scapula* 2.7, in *The Ante-Nicene Fathers*, vol. 3, ed Alexander Roberts and James Donaldson, rev. A. Cleveland Coxe (Grand Rapids, Mich.: Eerdmans, 1963), p. 106.
23. *Corpus Hermeticum* 24.3; cf. Ehrhardt, *Politische Metaphysik*, p. 277
24. Eusebius, *Life of Constantine* 1.44.1.

moniously into a new ideology of the empire, which gave the empire and its ruler a more effective metaphysical basis than the Roman empire ever had during its pagan period. It was only too easy to understand that, on the basis of this new "Christianized" ideology of rule, the *one God*, the *one empire*, and the *one ruler* also led to *one faith* and *one church*. Unfortunately it was all too quickly forgotten that the Christians themselves had once prayed for toleration in the face of reasons of state. Theodosius took the decisive step with his antipagan and anti-Jewish legislation. The historian Procopius sharply reproved Justinian for his fanatical zeal for unity of faith, since he stopped short of no crime for the sake of his allegedly noble goal: "For in his zeal *to gather all men into one Christian doctrine, he recklessly killed all who dissented,* and this too he did in the name of piety. For he did not call it homicide, when those who perished happened to be of a belief that was different from his own."[25]

Justinian's closing of the Platonic school of philosophy in Athens in 529 A. D.—after the school had existed for over nine hundred years—marked the end of pagan antiquity and the start of the Middle Ages. At the same time this "most Christian emperor" could confer on himself the entire heritage of the old pagan ruler ideology and assert that "God subordinates all laws to the *genius* of the emperor, which he sends to humankind as his personified law."[26]

Even Christ now became a projection of political power. The enthroned Christ in Byzantine mosaics, with purple and scepter, is also a representation of the earthly ruler of the world who holds sway over humanity in Christ's name. The portrayal of Christ as lawgiver, becoming more and more popular at that time, has a similar background. The earthly Jesus was no longer the dominant Christ figure. The suffering of Christ became a dogmatic embarrassment, as is shown, for example, by the theo-

---

25. Procopius, *Secret History* 13, trans. Richard Atwater (Ann Arbor, Mich.: University of Michigan Press, 1961), p. 68 (italics mine).

26. Justinian, *Novels* 105.2.4; see A. A. T. Ehrhardt, *Politische Metaphysik von Solon bis Augustin,* vol. 3, *Civitas Dei* (Tübingen: J. C. B. Mohr, 1969), p. 38.

paschite controversy over the possibility of suffering for the *one* divine-human person in fulfillment of his work of salvation. The battle was over the acknowledgment of the formula *unus ex trinitate passus est*: one of the persons of the Trinity actually suffered. Now even the preexistent Logos was no longer central, as he had been in the time of the Council of Nicea; much more the postincarnation, exalted, heavenly Christ in his power and glory was central, even though, according to the New Testament, this one "is not of this world" but, as the eschatological one, can only be anticipated in the faith and love of Christians. It is this heavenly Christ Eusebius is thinking of when he asserts that the Son of God was Constantine's comrade-in-arms in his victorious battle against Licinius. "It is the same 'great God and redeemer Jesus Christ' whose name Justinian later puts at the beginning of his novels, the supplements to his collection of Roman law, and in whose name Heraclius, another century later, crushes the Persians at Nineveh."[27]

By analogy the triumphal march of Islam in the seventh century had to be interpreted as a victory of the true prophet Mohammed over this political Christ. Perhaps it could be said that in the post-Constantinian "Christian metaphysics about the state" the ancient ruler ideology joined forces with Jewish theocracy. In this way the "kingdom that is not of this world," operative in faith, love, hope, and the powerlessness of suffering, was in danger of being lost.

Augustine (353–430 A. D.) was the first theologian who, in light of the new situation, thought through the relationship between empire and church in its total depth and complexity. In the Latin-speaking West the mistrust of Rome the world power, nourished by Christian apocalypticism, had remained more intense than in the Greek-speaking East, which bore the stamp of Origen's thought, although—or perhaps just because—the final period of persecution had been markedly less intense and shorter here than in the eastern part of the empire. In addition, in Rome

27. Werner Elert, *Der Ausgang der altkirchlichen Christologie* (Berlin: Lutherisches Verlagshaus, 1957), p. 31.

itself the old pagan opposition within the senatorial aristocracy maintained a considerable strength and consciously cultivated the old tradition about "eternal Rome." This was repressed for the first time through the victory of Theodosius over the rival emperor Eugenius in 394 A. D. One consequence of the apocalyptic tendencies in the thinking of Latin-speaking Christianity was its continuing predilection for chiliastic ideas.

In a conscious attempt to correct notions of that sort, Augustine, influenced by the commentary on the Apocalypse written by the Donatist Tyconius, applied the one-thousand-year reign of Christ with the saints, found in Revelation 20:6, no longer to an earthly kingdom of peace at the end of time but to the sixth age of the world, between the birth and parousia of Christ—that is, "to the time of the church."[28] During this one-thousand-year period from the time of Augustus until the final time of persecution prior to the return of Christ, Satan is bound (Rev. 20:2–3), that is, restrained from misleading the elect. This also provides opportunity for a mission to the whole world.

And yet, despite all its outward success, the church does not become the church triumphant but remains a pilgrim church. It is a "mixed body" (corpus permixtum) in which elect believers and the unfaithful live side by side like wheat and weeds (Matt. 13:24 ff.), to be separated only at the judgment. That is to say, Augustine can speak of the organized church as the "kingdom of Christ" (regnum Christi) only in a limited sense. This last is an entity that will appear in its completed form only on the last day. On the basis of Colossians 3:1–2 and Philippians 3:20, Augustine applies the "reigning with Christ" of Revelation 20:6 to the regeneration that comes in baptism, which fixes our eyes on our citizenship in heaven. The reign of Christ on earth is a stress-filled "militant kingdom [regnum militiae] in which we are still locked in battle with the enemy," that is, with sins and lusts.

---

28. Augustine, The City of God 20.7–10, trans. Marcus Dods (New York: Modern Library, 1950); cf. Ulrich Duchrow, Christenheit und Weltverantwortung (Stuttgart: E. Klett, 1970), pp. 259 ff.

Only the last day will bring the "most peaceful kingdom" (*regnum pacatissimum*).[29] "Consequently reigning with Christ means letting yourself be ruled by God and in this way attaining mastery over sin and its consequences."[30]   Justice and peace burst forth again and again as a fruit of this "reign of Christ," which thus also has political consequences, though these are, to be sure, only indirect. This realistic assessment of the reign of Christ in the world, which becomes visible only in faith's lively obedience, also sharpens Augustine's ability to see the demonic peril posed by the power of the state.

The occasion for his work *The City of God (De civitate Dei)*, antiquity's only great philosophy of history, was the pagan interpretation of the conquest and plundering of Rome by the Visigoths under Alaric in 410 A. D.   Christianity's opponents saw it as punishment from the ancient gods for apostasy to the new religion. The theologians of a "political Christ" had almost nothing to say in the face of this argument. For them the true God ultimately had to be on the side with the more powerful weapons. For Augustine, on the other hand, the earthly-political realm (*civitas terrena*) and the "city of God" (*civitas Dei*) were ultimately separate even though in this world they were to all appearances woven together inseparably. For the two stand under two opposing lords, God (or Christ) and the devil. Although all history is ultimately under the will of God and his plan of salvation, it still appears to be a continual battle.

This battle between the two domains has been going on since the beginning of creation. It goes back to the fall of the evil angels. Their tools are the great world empires: Assyria, along with the metropolis of Babylon, in the East, and Rome in the West. These great empires, if they do not operate in accord with justice (by Christian standards) are "great robber bands" (*magna latrocinia*).[31] Behind this expression we may see, with Ehrhardt,

29. *City of God* 20.9.
30. Duchrow, *Christenheit und Weltverantwortung*, p. 262.
31. *City of God* 4.4.

a polemical reversal of pagan polemics, "which since the days of Celsus had called the church a robber band."[32]

The history of Rome, that "tyrannical city" (*imperiosa civitas*)[33] continues to be dominated by "the lust for power" (*dominandi libido*, 3.14, 5.12, 5.19; cf. *dominandi cupido*, 15.7). This world power is basically a manifestation of humanity's original sins, self-love (*amor sui*), and conceit (*superbia*). Founded on a fratricide, Rome achieved power primarily through wars of conquest. For human happiness, on the other hand, it did precious little. Through it humanity was not at all unified. Rather through its size the gigantic empire developed into a hotbed of rebellion and civil war (3.6, 5.17, 19.7 and elsewhere). Political justice—insufficient even at its best—was practiced in a totally inadequate manner, and even when a certain measure was achieved, it could all be destroyed once again through conceit (14.9, toward the end). Thus the state was and remained "the manifestation of the power of antichrist"; for "the city of the ungodly . . . is without true justice" (19.24).

On the other hand, the state was still, "by God's grace, capable of improvement."[34] In Augustine's view this is shown by the development of the empire after Constantine, right up to Theodosius, who is for him its best representative (5.24–26). Of course the power of the state, for all its capacity for (a measure of) improvement, even when it was in Christian hands could increase the temporal prosperity of its subjects but could never attain the righteousness of the "city of God." The merging of both "cities" into one "Christian state" remained an inconceivable notion for him. Even the highest political good, peace, creates no true unity: "Enjoy the peace of Babylon. For from Babylon the people of God is so freed by faith that it meanwhile sojourns in its company."[35]

It stands in strange, and in its historical consequences totally

32. Ehrhardt, *Politische Metaphysik*, vol. 3, p. 40.
33. *City of God* 19.7.
34. Ehrhardt, *Politische Metaphysik*, vol. 3, p. 44.
35. *City of God* 19.26, p. 707 (translation modified).

disastrous contrast to this generally critical attitude toward the power of the state, that Augustine himself urges using the state's power against pagans and heretics. In his *On the Agreement of the Evangelists*[36] he defends, over against neoplatonic reproaches, the use of force by Christian rulers to suppress pagan cults and justifies this from the Old Testament, since he can produce no New Testament examples. Christian emperors should "make their power the handmaiden of the divine majesty."[37]

Following this idea to its logical conclusion, and breaking with earlier views, Augustine advocated the use of the power of the state against heretics and Donatists. In this connection he appealed, most regrettably, to the command a man giving a banquet issued to his servants in one of Jesus' parables (Luke 14:23): "Compel them to come in" (*coge intrare*; cf. epistles 93, 97, 100, 133, and often). The notion, common in antiquity, of the religious character of the state shows itself more clearly here than does theological reflection sharpened by the gospel. The emperor had to concern himself with the true religion of his subjects just as the father of a Roman family had to see to his family's true piety.[38] Because of these views Augustine can be called "the first apologist for an inquisition by the state."[39] This disastrous notion continued to be operative in the slogan of the Religious Peace of Augsburg in 1555, *cuius regio, eius religio* (the religion of the ruler determines the religion of his subjects), as well as in Lutheranism's concept that the ruler of a territory has supreme authority in the church.

It remains all the more significant that Augustine, through his sharp separation of the *civitas Dei* and the *civitas terrena*, put a stop to the threatened coalescence of the kingdom of God and the power of the state and made the metaphysical elevation of politi-

---

36. Augustine, *On the Agreement of the Evangelists* (*De consensu evangelistarum*) 1.24–25.

37. Reinhold Seeberg, *Lehrbuch der Dogmengeschichte*, vol. 2 (Darmstadt: Wissenschaftliche Buchgesellschaft, 1953 [reprint of 3rd ed. 1923]), p. 479 (commenting on *City of God*, 5.24, 26).

38. Duchrow, *Christenheit und Weltverantwortung*, p. 296.

39. Ehrhardt, *Politische Metaphysik*, vol. 3, p. 46.

cal power through a "political Christ" more difficult. The political danger in the West lay not in a new "emperor-God" but in
the church's political demand, based on the superiority of the
civitas Dei, that it has to prescribe the proper political actions to
the holders of the state's power. As a result of the fall of the
empire and of the changing dominions of the Germanic "barbarians," a vacuum ensued in which the church acquired a host of
new political functions. In addition she undertook—though no
doubt differently from the way Augustine had thought—"the
proper education of the human race"[40] At the same time, as the
representatives of ecclesiastical authority, the bishops more and
more became direct bearers of political power. In applying the
thousand-year reign in Revelation 20 to the church Augustine had
already understood the thrones and judges in v. 4 as the "rulers
through whom the church is now governed" (20.9). He himself
interpreted this as a reference to the apostolic power to bind and
loose mentioned in Matthew 18:18, that is, the power to forgive
sins,[41] but in later periods a political misinterpretation was also
possible. The most striking example of such political presump-
tion by the church is Pope Boniface VIII's bull *unam sanctam,*
from the year 1302, directed against Philip the Fair of France.
It claims that *both* swords mentioned in Luke 22:38, the secular
as well as the spiritual, are in the church's hands: "This one is
used *for* the church, the other *by* the church; that one through
the priest, this one through the kings and soldiers, at the command and by permission of the priests," for "the secular authority
must be subservient to the spiritual." The bull concludes with
the bombastic words: "We declare, assert, define, and proclaim
that for the sake of his salvation every human creature must be
completely submissive to the Roman pontiff."[42] It is no accident
that this exorbitant political claim began the downfall of ecclesi-

40. Augustine, *City of God* 10.14.
41. Duchrow, *Christenheit und Weltverantwortung,* pp. 262–63.
42. Heinrich Denzinger, ed., *Enchiridion symbolorum,* 30th ed. (Freiburg
im Breisgau: Herder, 1955), no. 469.

astical authority in the fourteenth century through the exile of the pope in Avignon and the ensuing schism.

To be sure, one dare not hold the bishop of Hippo, the greatest Latin church father, responsible for this subsequent radical politicization of the church. On the contrary, his work also awakened counterforces—as was true of his teaching on grace—which opposed this misuse of secular power by the highest ecclesiastical authority. Thus his work had a double effect, which Ehrhardt expresses clearly at the end of his great work on political metaphysics in the ancient world:

> His conviction that the visible church must and can defend peace and justice in this world transformed the church into a consciously political body that could organize into states the barbarians who had overrun and destroyed the Roman empire. But although the church was prepared to assume the roles of Joseph and Daniel (as examples of two statesmen who belonged to the *civitas Dei*), it continually refused to become a state itself, to create a theocracy such as Augustine had for all time clearly set before the church's eyes. It is this that stands behind the paradox of the gospel: "My kingdom is in your midst, my kingdom is not of this world."[43]

43. Ehrhardt, *Politische Metaphysik*, vol. 3, p. 51.

8

The Two Kingdoms
or the Reign of Christ

The coalescence of the church with the political powers, which, it is true, proceeded quite differently in the West under Augustine's influence than it did in Byzantium, was once more subjected to a fundamental theological challenge at the Reformation. Luther's violent protest was directed not least against the church's hierarchy and its self-understanding as a bearer of political and secular power. Luther directed the attack in a twofold way. First, he attacked the church's hierarchy and its privileges by means of the biblical teaching about the priesthood of all believers. Thus in 1523 he produced a treatise with the revolutionary title *That a Christian Assembly or Congregation Has the Right and Power to Judge All Teaching and to Call, Appoint, and Dismiss Teachers, Established and Proven by Scripture.*

Second, against the entanglement of secular-political and spiritual-ecclesiastical power, an entanglement that by his time had become inextricable, and also as a defense against the Enthusiasts, he unfolded the controversial *two kingdoms doctrine*. In broad strokes it looks something like this: God governs in this world in a twofold manner, in the "kingdom of God on the left and on the right hand."[1] The kingdom on the left hand, as described in Romans 13, is the kingdom of secular powers instituted by God—not the devil—among whom the sword holds sway. Over against this kingdom stands the reign of Christ, as the kingdom on the right hand, in which Christ operates through word and sacrament

1. Franz Lau, "Zwei-Reiche-Lehre," *Die Religion in Geschichte und Gegenwart*, vol. 6, ed. Kurt Galling (Tübingen: J. C. B. Mohr, 1962³), col. 1946.

and in which the commands in the Sermon on the Mount are unconditionally valid. For Christ's kingdom is spiritual. Through the gospel it produces faith and, thereby, eternal salvation. The secular kingdom is one of external power to keep order and inflict punishment, power that in a world dominated by sin preserves peace and prevents chaos. The two kingdoms dare not be combined. The kingdom of Christ can claim for itself no secular power; the secular kingdom is forbidden to encroach on the proclamation of the gospel in any way or to use any external force on the consciences of believers. Article 28.12 of the Augsburg Confession reads, "Therefore, the two authorities, the spiritual and the temporal, are not to be mingled or confused."[2]

To be sure, this concept of the two kingdoms was expressed in a variety of ways already in the Reformation era and in even more ways in later church history. It cannot be our task here to serve as a guide through the "labyrinth of the two kingdoms doctrine" (J. Heckel) or to go into the fine points in the distinction between the two kingdoms (*Reiche*) and the two ways of ruling (*Regimente*).

The current controversy in Protestant social ethics, with its slogans of the "two kingdoms doctrine" and the "royal reign of Christ," is in any case not merely a disagreement over the proper interpretation of Luther. It is just as surely a controversy over the modern problem of a "political theology," with both sides all too eagerly using the massive, and by no means systematically developed, work of Luther as a quarry from which to dig the foundation stones for their—at times only apparently—contradictory theses. Moreover, it is necessary to make a fundamental distinction between Luther's teaching, developed in the context of the Reformation controversy, on the fundamental difference between the kingdom of Christ and secular power, and its transformation in the new Lutheranism and liberalism of the nine-

2. *The Book of Concord*, trans. and ed. Theodore G. Tappert (Philadelphia: Fortress Press, 1959), p. 83. This translation renders the German version of the Augsburg Confession. The Latin version, also translated by Tappert, reads, *Non igitur commiscendae sunt potestates ecclesiastica et civilis* ("Therefore, ecclesiastical and civil power are not to be confused").

teenth and twentieth centuries. In the latter the kingdom of
Christ was limited more and more merely to inner spirituality of
mind and conscience while the all-powerful secular kingdom,
sanctioned as God's created order, was left to its manifold "autonomies." On this one-sided basis it was easy to postulate a kind
of harmony, established in advance, between the two kingdoms,
whereby the kingdom of Christ, precisely because of the sharp
separation between spiritual and secular, again and again had to
serve as justification and support for existing, thoroughly secular
power-relationships, especially since one could always invoke the
obedience toward the government called for in Romans 13.

Of course, a fundamental rejection of the two kingdoms doctrine by appeal to an all-encompassing "reign of Christ" was hardly
less dangerous. Karl Barth's picture in *The Christian Community
and the Civil Community* of two concentric circles around a
"common center," symbolizing that the "real Church must be the
model and prototype of the real State,"[3] overlooks, with its some-
what oversimplified analogy, the fundamental difference, indeed
opposition, of the two kingdoms that is expressed in the contra-
diction between the power of the word addressed to the conscience in the *regnum Christi* and the physical force used in the
regnum mundi. A direct, short-circuited appeal to the "reign of
Christ" could all too easily lead once again to the use and justification of political power and violence in the name of Christ, and
thus to a new theocratic form of the "political Christ."

Neither the two kingdoms doctrine nor the notion of a politically tangible "royal reign of Christ" is in itself immune to misuse
by established ruling powers or by revolutionary forces in the
process of establishing themselves. For instance, by appeal to the
separation of the two kingdoms, to the order of creation, and to
the political judgment of experts, some could justify such things
as the reintroduction of the death penalty, the election of a con-
servative party, a thoroughly free economy, or the production of

3. Karl Barth, "The Christian Community and the Civil Community," in
Against the Stream: Shorter Post-War Writings, 1946–52 (New York:
Philosophical Library, 1954), sec. 33, p. 48.

atomic weapons. Or, by appeal to the "reign of Christ," others could demand the socialization of productive capital, the Marxist-Leninist one-party system, revolution in the third world, and "victory in the people's war."

In the latter case the name of Christ is once again made into a label for a pseudo-religious, secular historical and redemptive myth. In the former case, on the other hand, through an appeal to the autonomy of law, economy, and politics, people give way to very human impulses such as the demand for vengeance, self-ishness, and fear. It is forgotten that through the prophetic and reconciling word and pious deed of Christians Christ wants to exercise his reign even in the (in itself evil) *regnum mundi*, that is, that he does not abandon the world to its autonomies.

We must, of course, distinguish the two kingdoms carefully, as Luther did, rather than mix them:

> Constantly I must pound in and squeeze in and drive in and wedge in this difference between the two kingdoms, even though it is written and said so often that it becomes tedious. The devil never stops cooking and brewing these two kingdoms into each other. In the devil's name the secular leaders always want to be Christ's masters and teach Him how He should run His church and spiritual government. Similarly, the false clerics and schismatic spirits always want to be masters, though not in God's name, and to teach people how to organize the secular government. Thus the devil is indeed very busy on both sides, and he has much to do. May God hinder him, amen, if we deserve it.[4]

Even today nothing is to be added to that; political powers desire to make the church compliant and to harness Christ to their wagon and, on the other hand, church leaders and theologians keep trying to use the state for their own purposes or else they imagine that the gospel can be expressed only politically now, since it has become identical with humanitarian and social

4. Martin Luther, "Commentary on Psalm 101," trans. Alfred von Rohr Sauer, in *Luther's Works*, vol. 13, *Selected Psalms* II, ed. Jaroslav Pelikan (St. Louis: Concordia Publishing House, 1956), pp. 194–95.

liberation. The problem is as serious now as it was at the Reformation.

But we dare not forget, in reference to this distinction, *that the two kingdoms cannot exist side by side as equals,* as one might perhaps view the relationship between church and state. Nor do they relate to one another simply as law and gospel or as the first and second articles of the creed. Rather it should be observed that the *regnum Christi* is qualitatively quite *different* and at the same time *more comprehensive,* that it determines not only the life of Christians but ultimately even the meaning and future of the world. In it is found the limit and end of the *regnum mundi,* which, although it rests on divine decree, has since Augustine borne within itself the double nature of the *civitas terrena,* the earthly realm, and the *civitas diaboli,* the devil's sphere of influence.

On the other hand, the reign of Christ in this world, in history, frequently presents itself in an outwardly very questionable, indeed pitiful manner. Here only the believing, praying, suffering, prophetically admonishing and ministering church as the body of Christ is its representative and executor, a church that precisely today all too often fails, suffers attack, and is therefore frequently despised. It is, nevertheless, in such failure and under all the attacks it experiences, closer to the Lord of the church than was the triumphal church at the time of a Justinian in Byzantium or a Boniface VIII in Rome.

The means by which the reign of Christ is actualized in the church is above all the word, which strikes the conscience of the hearer, "convinces" him, and thus evokes "faith" that incorporates him into the community of believers, transforms his life and effects within the congregation the fruit of the Spirit, that is, specific actions. By these very actions the *regnum Christi* interpenetrates the *regnum mundi,* and, beyond that, indirectly asserts its claim of authority over against it. For Christians have secular callings, not least also in the service of the state itself. Already in the fourth century the church father Basil the Great, who stressed over against the imperial prefect that "the mark of a Christian is not his station in life but his faith," appealed to Christians not to shun the office of censor, "since the Lord has wished the district of Ibora not to be in the power of hucksters, nor the taking of its census to be like a slave-market, but that each man shall be enrolled in a just manner, accept the task . . ."[5]

The confessions from the Reformation period expressed this demand quite emphatically over against the Enthusiasts: "Christians may without sin occupy civil offices or serve as princes and judges, render decisions and pass sentence according to imperial and other existing laws, punish evildoers with the sword, engage in just wars, serve as soldiers, buy and sell, take required oaths, possess property, be married, etc."[6]

Of course, in a changed situation right here in Germany and in view of the increasing proximity in which humanity lives, approaching more and more antiquity's ideal of the cosmopolis, one is more reserved about individual formulations such as *supplicia iure constituere, iure bellare, militare*—"to award just punishments, to engage in just wars, to serve as soldiers." On the other hand, through the political change from the patriarchal, authoritarian state prevalent in Luther's time to pluralistic democracy, participation in and responsibility for the *regnum mundi* in its varied forms on the part of Christians, individually as well as corporately, has become very much greater, indeed has become absolutely necessary. The government today is no longer an alien entity inescapably imposed by God. Rather it is a multi-

5. Basil, *The Letters* 4.299, trans. Roy J. Deferrari, Loeb Classical Library, (Cambridge, Mass.: Harvard University Press, 1934), p. 217.

6. Augsburg Confession 16.2, p. 37 (the Tappert translation of the German version. The Latin text, also translated by Tappert, reads: *Christianis liceat gerere magistratus, exercere iudicia, iudicare res ex imperatoriis et aliis praesentibus legibus, supplicia iure constituere, iure bellare, militare, lege contrahere, tenere proprium, iurare postulantibus magistratibus, ducere uxorem, nubere*—"It is right for Christians to hold civil office, to sit as judges, to decide matters by the imperial and other existing laws, to award just punishments, to engage in just wars, to serve as soldiers, to make legal contracts, to hold property, to swear oaths when required by magistrates, to marry, to be given in marriage").

layered complex of jurisdictions, as a rule elected by the citizens, jurisdictions that should have as their sole concern the welfare of all and therefore need constructive criticism as well as obedience.

The self-evident participation of Christians in secular callings and in the service of the state does not yet sufficiently express, of course, Christ's claim of authority in the *regnum mundi.* Therefore the Reformation confessions stress the central point of departure from which this is to happen: "The Gospel . . . requires . . . that everyone, *each according to his own calling, manifest Christian love and genuine good works in his station of life*"[7] In this context obedience toward the government is also required, though to be sure with the decisive qualification, "in all that can be done without sin. But when commands of the civil authority cannot be obeyed without sin, we must obey God rather than men (Acts 5:29)."[8]

In the light of the experiences of the last sixty years the concluding statement becomes crucially important. It makes it impossible to justify compliance to an unjust command by appealing to a "state of emergency" No one should go against his conscience. The picture, so popular today, of Luther as a "lackey of the princes" is a distortion. In a time of lackeys to party and career, in which the worst abuses and crimes are cloaked with the mantle of solidarity and "anything for the good of the party," no one can make this particular accusation against Luther. He expressed himself much more forcefully against the princes than is usual with our ideologues, who are so locked into their party that they whitewash the sins of their own side and see only those of the opposition. Luther not only lashed out with bitter polem-

---

7. Augsburg Confession 16.5, p. 38 (the Tappert translation following the German version. The Latin says that the gospel requires of Christians *in talibus ordinationibus exercere caritatem*—"the exercise of love in these ordinances" [Tappert translation; italics mine]).

8. Augsburg Confession 16.6, p. 38 (the Tappert translation following the German version. The Latin reads, *nisi cum iubent peccare; tunc enim magis debent oboedire Deo quam hominibus*—"except when commanded to sin, for then they ought to obey God rather than men" [Tappert translation]).

ics against "the high and the mighty," but also urged Christians, and especially pastors, to be prepared to resist injustice, of course *sine vi sed verbo* ("without human power simply by the Word"): "One should endure injustice and violence, but not in silence. For a Christian should bear witness to the truth and die for the truth . . ."[9]

Here we encounter the basis on which a Christian, uniting his existence under faith and his secular life, allows the Lordship of Christ to operate also in the *regnum mundi*: he proclaims it *by serving*, that is, by works of love and by prophetic protest against injustice, even if—rather, precisely when—this causes him to suffer. Such protest can be made by word as well as deed. Both the prophets and Jesus employed provocative symbolic action. Whether and to what degree in this kind of action the boundary of physical violence may be crossed is ultimately a question for the individual to decide personally according to his or her conscience as well as a question for critical self-examination by whole groups. We should not allow ourselves to make these decisions too lightly today, since all over the world such violence is glorified by the most diverse groups as justified and necessary and, at the same time, since the catastrophic results of such violence are becoming more and more apparent.

The ancient church might serve as an example for us in this regard more than it has in the past. How great the perplexity can be, how difficult the individual decision, may be seen in the way of Bonhoeffer, which finally led beyond political opposition motivated by faith into martyrdom. It could be a good sign if we as Christians today have become more sensitive on this point than earlier generations were, and if we have also maintained an awareness of the problem of "structural violence." It will be the task of a Christian to work above all toward the control and reduction of violence. Only in such "action that grows out of faith" (Rom. 14:23) will the separation of the two kingdoms be continually overcome.

9. *D. Martin Luthers Werke* 28.361.37–38 (Weimar, 1883–1970), pp. 37–39 (hereafter cited as *WA*).

In the confession that accompanies Luther's treatise concerning Christ's supper (1528), out of which the Augsburg Confession grew, it is the Reformer's view that

> above these three institutions and orders [the office of priest, the estate of marriage, and civil government] is the common order of Christian love, in which one serves not only the three orders, but also serves every needy person in general with all kinds of benevolent deeds, such as feeding the hungry, giving drink to the thirsty, forgiving enemies, praying for all men on earth, suffering all kinds of evil on earth, etc.[10]

In *The Freedom of a Christian* Luther expressed in a singular manner this dialectic in the life of a Christian who is by faith a free citizen of Christ's kingdom (cf. Phil. 3:20) and a herald of Christ obliged to serve in this world. He develops in this treatise the twofold introductory thesis: "A Christian is a perfectly free lord of all, subject to none. A Christian is a perfectly dutiful servant of all, subject to all."[11] The power of Christ is visible and tangible in this world only when the Christian, "free from all works, . . . in this liberty [empties] himself, [and takes] upon himself the form of a servant . . . to serve, help, and in every way deal with his neighbor as he sees that God through Christ has dealt and still deals with him."[12] Indeed Luther can say that a Christian "becomes Christ" to his neighbor: "I will therefore give myself as a Christ to my neighbor, just as Christ offered himself to me; I will do nothing in this life except what I see is necessary, profitable, and salutary to my neighbor, since through faith I have an abundance of all good things in Christ."[13]

This proclamation of the lordship of Christ by serving one's neighbor has reference not only to individuals but applies also to groups, congregations, religious communities—indeed to the en-

10. "Confession Concerning Christ's Supper, 1528," trans. Robert Fischer, in *Luther's Works*, vol. 37, *Word and Sacrament* III, ed. Robert Fischer and Helmut T. Lehmann (Philadelphia: Fortress, 1961), p. 365 (WA 26.505).
11. *The Freedom of a Christian*, trans. W. A. Lambert and rev. Harold J. Grimm, in *Luther's Works*, vol. 31, *Career of the Reformer* I, ed. Harold J. Grimm and Helmut T. Lehmann (Philadelphia: Fortress, 1957), p. 344.
12. Ibid., p. 366.
13. Ibid., p. 367 (WA 7.35–36).

tire church. On this foundation one can erect not only a Christian ethic for the individual but also responsible behavior in the field of social ethics, as Ernst Wolf especially has emphasized.[14] He has shown that on this basis even the concept of discipleship, too long misunderstood as *imitatio Christi* (the imitation of Christ), gains a new profile. He points in this context to the Reformer's bold remarks in the theses for the doctoral examination of Hieronymus Weller:

> For when we have Christ, then we shall easily make laws and judge everything justly. Beyond that we shall make new decalogues, as Paul does in all his epistles, and Peter [as well], and especially Christ in the gospel. And these decalogues are clearer than the decalogue of Moses, just as the countenance of Christ is clearer than the face of Moses. . . . How much more Paul or a mature Christian full of the Holy Spirit can set up a decalogue and judge everything in the best way possible.[15]

The power of Christians lies in the "freedom that grows out of their faith," through which, their consciences bound solely by the command and promise of their Lord, they perform loving service in their calling, in the workaday world, as the particular situation in which they find themselves dictates.

This is probably also the background for an understanding of the still so controversial second thesis of the Barmen Declaration of 1934, directed against the German Christian Movement:

> "But of him are ye in Christ Jesus, who of God is made unto us wisdom, and righteousness, and sanctification, and redemption" (1 Cor. 1:30). Just as Jesus Christ is the pledge of forgiveness of all our sins, just so—and with the same earnestness—is he also God's mighty claim on our whole life; in him we encounter a joyous liberation from the godless claims of this world to free and thankful service to his creatures. We repudiate the false teaching that there are areas of our life in which we belong not to Jesus

14. Ernst Wolf, *Peregrinatio*, vol. 2, *Studien zur reformatorischen Theologie, zum Kirchenrecht und zur Sozialethik* (Munich: Kaiser-Verlag, 1965), pp. 225 ff.

15. Ibid., p. 239 (cf. *WA* 39.1, p. 47).

Christ but another lord, areas in which we do not need justification and sanctification through him.[16]

In Christians' "free and thankful service" to God's creation by word and deed, and therein alone, Christ's power becomes visible in the world and actually comprehensible. The central question addressed to us Christians today is, How does this service happen in the proper way as a service of love guided by conscience, a service which at the same time constitutes "true worship," which does not identify with "this world" all too quickly, but rather, maintaining a critical distance to itself as well as to the ruling powers, seeks to "discover what the will of God is" (Rom. 12:1–2)?

That the attempt to construct a theological ethic for the political sphere on the foundation of the second thesis of the Barmen Declaration will be no easy task is shown by the statement on the political task of the Christian community issued by the theological commission of the Evangelische Kirche der Union.[17] For it came to no one-dimensional conclusion, as, for instance, E. Dinkler's noteworthy objections show.[18]

More than ever the church needs open discussion of the question of power, for this has become urgent for us both in the political and the social sphere. The discussion needs to take place without repressive group pressure, without threats and fear, and this also means without too hasty an identification with the ruling political powers and programs, but rather in a spirit of tolerance with a willingness to seek agreement. Precisely when we Christians, in our dialogue with the "mighty" of all shades of opinion, are objective and critical, which in some circumstances would mean troublesome, are we fulfilling our mission to love

16. John Leith, ed., *Creeds of the Churches* (Garden City, N.Y.: Doubleday, 1963), p. 520 (translation reprinted from Franklin Littell, *The German Phoenix* [Garden City, N.Y.: Doubleday, 1960]).

17. A. Burgsmüller, ed., *Zum politischen Auftrag der christlichen Gemeinde, Barmen II. Votum des Theologischen Ausschusses der EKU* (Gütersloh, 1974) (with contributions by H.-G. Geyer, J. Hamel, and others).

18. Ibid., pp. 259 ff., 281–82.

them.   In that context we dare not forget, of course, that in numerous countries today the church is once again a suffering, outwardly powerless body, and that the possibility for that sort of open and critical discussion is by no means self-evident. Therefore, when theological groups, in response to the demand to follow the political party line, minimize or suppress an awareness of the suffering of their brothers in far-off parts of the world— who speaks, for example, of the fate of the church in Albania or in South or North Korea?—they show, despite their cheap talk about "freedom from domination," that deep down they have again submitted to mighty political powers.

The obvious power of Christ in our world today is tied inseparably to our speaking and acting as Christians, and his powerlessness to our silence and failure to act.   This applies to the whole church, for the community of believers, as the body of Christ, represents its Lord here and now: "So we are ambassadors for Christ" (2 Cor. 5:20).

Summary

The following ten points summarize our reflections, which have encompassed a broad span of periods and issues:

1. If we proceed from Max Weber's definition quoted in the Introduction, then we would say that the power of Christ is able to "carry out [its] own will despite resistance," but that this in no case can happen through external coercion, but only through genuine persuasion of the person addressed, *sine vi humana sed verbo*—"without human power, simply by the word."

2. Jesus' power was displayed as he proclaimed God's lordship over humanity. This happened in his announcement of God's love to all the "godless" and lost. Through his authoritative word and his helping deed he gave them a new, meaningful life.

3. Therefore this power of Jesus stands in irreconcilable opposition to every metaphysical glorification of human, political powers, and in the same way to the claim of a theocracy that by appeal to God's lordship wants only to press its own demand for power.

4. As a logical consequence of his outwardly offensive and unavailing announcement of God's lordship Jesus goes to his death. His suffering becomes the sign of God's solidarity with the powerlessness of the righteous in their suffering, and thus the foundation of the life-creating power of the gospel.

5. The early church's messengers relied solely on the power of this word and on the risen Lord's promise that stood behind it. Jesus' way of suffering gave them assurance of reconciliation with God and at the same time shaped the external form of their ministry.

6. There existed from the beginning in the early church a dialectic between the apostolic authority established through appearances of the risen Lord and the free charism of the Spirit. Adherence to the truth of the gospel was the standard by which each was evaluated. Even after the institutionalization of ecclesiastical authority the charismatic corrective survived.

7. When the persecutions began, the Christians still remained loyal to the political authorities. Nevertheless they emphatically had to reject emperor worship. They lived in the hope that after a final intensification of ungodly hubris Christ would transform the world and establish his now-hidden kingdom for all to see. Jesus' passion gave them the certainty that the kingdom of this world, despite all the persecutions, was deprived of its power through the kingdom of Christ.

8. Together with this, however, the expectation developed that the entire Roman empire would convert to the Christian faith. With the inauguration of the Constantinian era this hope appeared to be fulfilled. To be sure, through its participation in the power of the state there arose for the church the new threat that it would lead to a metaphysical overvaluing of a Christian empire, and that with the aid of the power of the state it could compel acceptance of its message. The "political Christ" became the bearer of a new ideology of the empire.

9. The Reformation not only broke with the power claims of the ecclesiastical hierarchy but also attempted through the two kingdoms doctrine—which evolved from Augustine and today is much debated—to abolish the unholy mingling of secular and spiritual power. Thereby, of course, the danger arose of the complete separation of the two realms, whereby the politicosocial realm would be left to its own autonomies.

10. In contrast to that, Luther and the confessions from the Reformation era stressed that the lordship of Christ extends into the secular realm through service by Christians. The power of Christ takes shape through the true worship of Christians in the everyday world. Here is the foundation for responsible ethical living by Christians in their secular callings.

note two principal questions

Title is too limited — the book
is in fact a broad study
of the - Roman relations, etc.

John 18 — See p. 49!

errata — p. 53

gems — p. 18